WES DERVINS

W9-CUW-300

Peace and the War Industry

Peace and the War Industry

Edited by
KENNETH E. BOULDING

*Trans-***action** Books

Published by
Aldine Publishing Company

The essays in this book originally appeared
in *Trans-*action Magazine

First Printing — January 1970
Second Printing — September 1970

Copyright © 1970 by Transaction, Inc.
All Rights Reserved
Printed in the United States of America

TA Book-11
Library of Congress Catalog Number: 71-96133

Contents

Preface

However diverse their attitudes and interpretations may sometimes be, social scientists are now entering a period of shared realization that the United States—both at home and abroad—has entered a crucial period of transition. Indeed, the much burdened word "crisis" has now become a commonplace among black militants, Wall Street lawyers, housewives, and even professional politicians.

For the past six years, *Trans*-action magazine has dedicated itself to the task of reporting the strains and conflicts within the American system. But the magazine has done more than this. It has pioneered in social programs for changing the society, offered the kind of analysis that has permanently restructured the terms of the "dialogue" between peoples and publics, and offered the sort of prognosis that makes for real alterations in social and political policies directly affecting our lives.

The work done in the pages of *Trans*-action has crossed

disciplinary boundaries. This represents much more than simple cross-disciplinary "team efforts." It embodies rather a recognition that the social world cannot be easily carved into neat academic disciplines. That, indeed, the study of the experience of blacks in American ghettos, or the manifold uses and abuses of agencies of law enforcement, or the sorts of overseas policies that lead to the celebration of some dictatorships and the condemnation of others, can best be examined from many viewpoints and from the vantage points of many disciplines.

This series of books clearly demonstrates the superiority of starting with real world problems and searching out practical solutions, over the zealous guardianship of professional boundaries. Indeed, it is precisely this approach that has elicited enthusiastic support from leading American social scientists for this new and dynamic series of books.

The demands upon scholarship and scientific judgment are particularly stringent, for no one has been untouched by the current situation. Each essay republished in these volumes bears the imprint of the author's attempt to communicate his own experience of the crisis. Yet, despite the sense of urgency these papers exhibit, the editors feel that many have withstood the test of time, and match in durable interest the best of available social science literature. This collection of *Trans*-action articles, then, attempts to address itself to immediate issues without violating the basic insights derived from the classical literature in the various fields of social science.

The subject matter of these books concerns social changes that have aroused the long-standing needs and present-day anxieties of us all. These changes are in organizational life styles, concepts of human ability and intelligence, changing patterns of norms and morals, the relationship of social conditions to physical and biological environments, and in the status of social science with national policy making.

This has been a decade of dissident minorities, massive shifts in norms of social conduct, population explosions and urban expansions, and vast realignments between nations of the world. The social scientists involved as editors and authors of this *Trans*-action series have gone beyond observation of these critical areas, and have entered into the vital and difficult tasks of explanation and interpretation. They have defined issues in a way making solutions possible. They have provided answers as well as asked the right questions. Thus, this series should be conceived as the first collection dedicated not to the highlighting of social problems alone, but to establishing guidelines for social solutions based on the social sciences.

THE EDITORS
Trans-action

The Deadly Industry: War and the International System

KENNETH E. BOULDING

We have now had reasonably accurate national accounts for the United States for nearly forty years; that is, for the effective lifetimes of those who are now getting into positions of power and important decision-making. The importance of this cumulative record is hard to over-estimate. It does for economics what the painstaking collection of long-time observation of the movements of the planets did for astronomy. It gives us a framework within which everything can be seen in proportion. One suspects that most errors in judgement and decision arise because the world is perceived in terms of what is salient rather than what is in high proportion. It is only the collection of records of this kind, however, that enable us to see what the proportions are.

In dealing with the proportions of the economy, the first question one must ask is, what is the total, what is 100 percent? The Gross National Product is often taken as the

1

measure of the total size of the economy. This, however, is unsatisfactory, especially in a period of unemployment, because it does not measure the capacity of the system, but only what is realized. It is necessary, therefore, to develop a concept of what I am calling the "Gross Capacity Product," which represents what the gross product would have been if there had been no unemployment. The measurement of this is not easy, and for the purposes of the present analysis a very rough measure has been devised, in which we simply take the Gross National Product and increase it by the proportion of the labor force unemployed. The Gross Capacity Product is then defined by the following formula:

$$\text{Gross Capacity Product} = \text{Gross National Product} \times \frac{100}{100 - e}$$

where e is the proportion of the labor force unemployed. This measure is subject to two errors which operate in opposite directions, and hopefully may be subject to the law of benevolently countervailing error. The first is that the unemployed would presumably be less productive than the employed labor force if they were actually employed, so that the above measure exaggerates the Gross Capacity Product by an amount which depends on how low is the productivity of the unemployed. On the other hand, the official unemployment figure underestimates unemployment because it does not take account of underemployment, part-time work and so on. The Gross National Product also underestimates the contribution of housewives and non-marketable labor. These two factors would make our measure of the Gross Capacity Product too small. One may hope, though, that these two errors in opposite directions will cancel each other out, and our measure may be taken as at least a simple index which may not be wholly accurate in the more extreme years.

Figure 1, then, shows the history of the last thirty-nine years in terms of the proportionate structure of the Gross Capacity Product. We see the depth of the Great Depression in the unrealized product—almost 25 percent in 1933. We see also that the New Deal was a failure in terms of its major objective to solve the unemployment problem, even though it had some important long-run spinoffs, in terms of Social Security and the like. The recovery from the bottom of '33 was very slow. Even in '37 the unrealized product was still 15 percent, and the depression of '38 pushed us back almost to the position at the beginning of '32; even by 1940 we had only gotten back to the position of 1936. The losses here are enormous and represent something like two whole years' product in the twelve years from 1929 to 1941.

We see the Second World War vividly as an enormous expansion of national defense, from under 1 percent of the Gross Capacity Product during the depression to over 40 percent in 1942, 1943, and 1944. We see very vividly the source of what I have sometimes called the "great American myth"—that only a large war industry can save us from depression, for in the memory of those who lived through this period, this was, in fact, their experience. The war did reduce unemployment to virtually zero, and it was paid for half out of the unemployment that might have been there otherwise and about half by reduction in the other elements of the system, especially civilian government, gross private domestic investment, and personal consumption.

We next see the Great Disarmament of 1945 and '46. It is odd that this has left so little impression on the American consciousness. It was achieved with unemployment never rising above 3 percent and with astonishingly little dislocation. Its history has never been properly written, but it is one of the most extraordinary episodes in all of

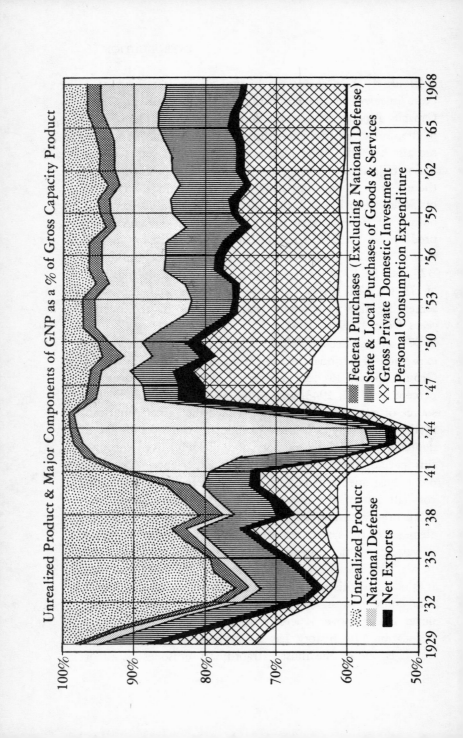

Unrealized Product & Major Components of GNP as a % of Gross Capacity Product economic history. Here is the transfer of almost a third of the economic activity of a large and very complex society from the war industry into civilian purposes. It is done in little over a year and with an incredibly small amount of disruption.

We then see the first cold war rearmament from 1950 into the Korean War, which reached its maximum in 1953 and continued through the fifties into the sixties, with national defense occupying from 8 to 10 percent of the Gross Capacity Product. This is a very marked structural change from the thirties and is perhaps among the three major structural changes in the American economy in this period, the other two being the decline of agriculture and the decline of the whole private sector of the economy, especially personal consumption expenditure, in the face of expanding government. We should note, however, the period from '63 to '65, when national defense as a proportion of Gross Capacity Product declined and unemployment likewise declined. From '65 to '68 we see the expansion due to the Vietnam War, which from the American point of view is almost frighteningly small.

An extraordinarily interesting feature of the last twenty years has been the stability in the proportionate structure in the American economy in many ways. Personal consumption structure was squeezed by the expansion of the military, but has remained virtually stable as a proportion of the Gross Capacity Product, at close to 60 percent ever since 1951. Gross private domestic investment, likewise, has been extraordinarily stable, apart from a small cyclical fluctuation, a good part of which is in inventory. The total government sector is, likewise, astonishingly stable, and one of the striking features of the sixties is the way in which the civilian government proportion of the economy (both state, local and federal) rose in response to the declining proportion of national defense. It must be remembered, at all times, that these are proportionate, not absolute, figures, and that in this period, of course, the Gross Capacity Product itself rose, in fact more than doubled in real terms. The contrast between the period of great instability in the proportionate structure before, say, 1946 and the period of relative stability since, is almost certainly beginning to have an effect on our national attitudes and our perception of the world.

Paradoxically enough, one of the principal consequences of full employment is the reappearance of scarcity. The critical question here is what goes down when national defense expenditure goes up by a dollar. If what goes down is simply unemployment, as in the "great American myth," then national defense is virtually costless in real terms. If, however, we have approximately full employment, or at least moderately full employment, as we have had for the last twenty years, suddenly scarcity reasserts itself, and it becomes very clear that a dollar on the military is a dollar off somebody else, and then the question becomes of great importance—"Who is the somebody else?" This is a question unfortunately that is by no means easy to answer, for components of the economy may go up and down for a great variety of reasons. We cannot simply assume that if something goes down when the military goes up that this was a cause-and-effect relationship. If, for instance, we look at the components of personal consumption expenditure, we find that food and clothing have gone down quite sharply as a proportion of the Gross Capacity Product, but this is because we are getting richer, and it is a well-known law in economics, which even has a name—"Engle's Law" (the singular Engle, not the plural Engles). If we were to bring the war industry down to the proportionate level of the thirties, assuming that we maintained full employment, as with modern techniques it is fairly easy to do, it is not altogether easy to say what would expand. The evidence suggests that personal consumption would expand and so would civilian government, but in what proportions it is not easy to say, and indeed this may well depend on the particular policies and sentiments which happen to be in operation at the time. If we are in a Galbraithian mood, as we seem to have been in the last ten years or so, with the remarkable expansion of civilian government, we may expect this expansion to continue. On the other hand, if we are in a more private mood, we are well aware that the biggest bite out of the economy which the war industry imposes is the bite out of personal consumption expenditure, which is now only 60 percent of the Gross Capacity Product, as against 72 percent in 1929. In such a case, the pressure may be for tax reduction and even budget deficits which will expand the private sector and the personal sector.

There are some interesting, but equally unanswerable, political questions involved in this rather sketchy economic analysis. The important question here in the face of an increasing consciousness of scarcity is what kind of political coalitions are likely to form against the war industry. Coalitions tend to form among people who have a common sense that their particular ox is being gored, even though they may have very different oxen. The political coalition that is most likely to form against the war industry would seem to be, from this analysis, a rather odd combination of left and right, the people who feel that the war industry is biting into civilian government and especially, what is not shown in the figure, into transfers, and on the other hand, the people, who feel that the real bite is out of the private household sector. The combination of little old ladies in tennis shoes and bright-eyed left-wing bureaucrats may sound too implausible even to mention, but stranger things may have happened, and this would seem to be where the combination of economic interests lies.

Behind all this argument lies an assumption that the national defense component is politically flexible in response to domestic demands. Economists, on the whole, have regarded national defense as essentially exogenous (that is, determined by forces completely outside the economic system and especially the domestic economic system). This is the myth of military necessity, which the military, of course, is not slow to foster. In fact, however, it is a myth, as the votes for appropriations for national defense, which essentially determine the size of the war industry, depend on a great variety of circumstances, and especially on the current concept of the national image and the national interest. One of the important things that seems to be happening at the moment is the realization that the national interest is a variable, not a constant of the system, and that it is, in fact, simply what the nation is interested in. All organizations, and the nation is no exception, are interested in survival, but the nation is interested in many other things beside this, and if national defense were directed solely at survival it would almost certainly be very much less than it is now and of a very different composition.

The rise in the proportion of the Gross Capacity Product occupied by the war industry is partly a reflection of a real change in the international system itself which has brought us all so uncomfortably close together, but it is also a reflection in the change in the national image, from a nation lying somewhat on the periphery of the international system (which was the way we visualized ourselves even up to the Second World War), to a nation which is central in the international system. This is what I have sometimes called the "mantle of Elijah complex," the image being that the mantle of the British Empire has fallen on us. This particularly seems to have been the case with the Democrats. Both Acheson and Rusk had a strong sense of having been covered with the mantle of Elijah, which came fluttering down from the British as they proceeded to descend from the cloudy heights of great powerdom and built themselves a comfortable little welfare state on terra firma. The British abandonment of the image of being a great power was partly a result of the rising costs of being a power, but also a result of the increasing domestic pressures, especially on the government sector. We see something of the same thing happening in this country in the last fifteen years, at least in the slow encroachment of civilian government on national defense, which is particularly noticeable up till 1965. The criticism of the Vietnam War, which is surely the most unpopular war in American history, is a result not only of its uselessness in terms of any conceivable national interest, but also, I think, because of the reawakened sense of "scarcity" and the feeling that the Vietnam War was pressing on much more urgent domestic priorities, especially in the government sector.

In conclusion, then, the international system can be thought of as a certain segment of the total world social system. And the war industry, which may be defined as that part of the economy purchased by military budgets, comprises a very large part of the international system. In terms of the world economy, the world war industry is of the order of 5 to 10 percent of the world product. The international system outside the war industry—the state departments, foreign offices, diplomats and so on—occupies a very tiny fraction of the total economy. The international system occupies a larger proportion of the communications system, such as history books and newspapers. It has a saliency that makes its quantitative impact on the totality of human life hard to measure. For example, it is doubtful that more than 10 percent of the total output of communications deals with the international system in terms of sheer quantity, but it seems to loom larger than that, perhaps because it is subject to sudden ups and downs and it is also perceived as very dangerous.

In the United States the war industry has varied from 0.6 percent of the Gross National Product to about 42 percent over the last forty years, and is now running at about 9 percent, of which about 3 percent is the Vietnam War. The war industry is a much larger part of the political system than it is of the economic system. Thus, in the United States the war industry occupies some 41 percent of the total government sector of the economy, including federal, state and local. The international system must take a large proportion of the time of the President, although a much smaller proportion of the time of Congress.

There is a widespread feeling, which most of the papers in this collection reflect, that the international system is dangerous and expensive, that its legitimacy has been declining and that an ardent search for a better solution to this problem is very much in order. The scientific revolution has made an enormous impact on the international system and has, I believe, made it obsolete. The international system is the major part of the total social system where threat predominates as a social organizer. In internal political systems, we have what might be called a legitimated threat-submission system, in which people pay their taxes and submit to laws, partly because they approve of doing so in principle, and partly because, if they don't, they will get into trouble. The international system is characterized primarily by deterrence (that is, a threatcounterthreat system). "If you do something nasty to me, I will do something nasty to you." The principal product of the war industry is threat capability, that is, the capability of carrying out threats by being able to produce negative commodities or "bads." The threat system has a much lower horizon of development than the exchange system, in which we persuade others to do something for us by offering them goods rather than threatening to give them "bads." The main difficulty with the threat system is that it is most effective when the threats are not carried out (that is, when they are credible enough to influence behavior), but unless they are occasionally carried out they cease to be credible. The carrying out of a threat, though, is often more costly to the threatener than it is to the victim. This makes the whole economics of the threat system very peculiar.

One of the real problems of the international system has been the absence of adequate theory. We have had a pretty good theory of the exchange system for a long time now. This is economics. The theory of the threat system, and especially the theory of the interaction between the threat system and the exchange system, is still in a rather primitive stage.

I am not suggesting, of course, that these economic considerations are a sufficient, or even a prime, explanation of the sort of things that are going on and which are reflected in the articles in this volume. The international system itself is primarily a political system in the sense that it is based much more on threat than on exchange. The interrelations between the exchange system and the threat system, however, have suddenly become of great interest and, one suspects, of much greater importance than they have been in the past, though there are theoretical problems here that we are still very far from having solved. These one can recommend with great enthusiasm to the social scientists whose work in this area will undoubtedly continue to be published in *Trans*-action.

The papers of this volume are topical and they represent applied social science rather than basic theory, though some of them represent rigorous empirical work. Some readers, indeed, may regard them as merely straws in the wind. Nevertheless, it is a big wind that is blowing, and it suggests that a radical transformation in our whole set of perceptions about the international system may not be far away. Because of their topical nature they have been arranged in chronological order, dating from 1964 to 1969. Anyone who wants to know what has been going on in these years at the frontiers of thought and research about the international system, somewhat removed from the established citadels of the conventional wisdom, will find these papers most rewarding.

University of Colorado
Boulder, Colorado

Paradoxes of the Warfare State

ELWIN H. POWELL

Today the preparation for war is the central activity of the modern nation. The world "spends" over $100 billion a year on war, half coming from the United States, a fourth from the Soviet Union, with the remainder shared by other major powers. In the United States the annual expenditures for defense procurement alone are, according to a U. S. Congressional committee, "twice as large as the total net farm income of the nation ... almost twice as large as the total U. S. expenditure for public education." The 1964 defense budget of 56 billion will consume 65 percent of the tax dollar, provide employment for over 10 percent of the labor force and generate some $110 billion in economic activity.

When then are the social consequences of this massive "war" effort? In the early 1950's Harold Lasswell could foresee a "thickening atmosphere of suspicion" as the superstates each became monolithic and as the democratic process died " by slow strangulation." Yet insofar as the war operation has involved a real conflict, not merely an imposture, it has brought certain beneficial changes in "world society." The Soviet need to prosecute the "cold war" is dissolving its own "iron curtain" just as the American response to the Soviet challenge has broken down our tradition and practice of isolationism. Contrary to George Orwell's anticipation, the two systems have not remained "inviolate within their own boundaries." And conflict, as Lewis Coser has pointed out "establishes relations where none may have existed before."

When neither side can annihilate the other and still continue to function as a unit, then conflict is often transmuted into accommodation, and in time accommodation becomes cooperation. Faint hints of the subsiding of world tension are even now apparent and could bring about a wilting of the superstates; indeed, signs of the breakup of war-created alliances of both East and West are already discernible.

The warfare state calls into being its own antithesis, perhaps leading eventually to a new synthesis which none of us can now foresee. The growth of the military-industrial complex has generated counter-currents which seem to contradict the very premises of the garrison state. These unintended consequences of war preparation can be viewed as a series of interrelated paradoxes.

Paradox I: The military-industrial complex does not engender militarism: "Militarism is not so much the propensity to wage war," writes Hans Speier, "as the organization of the civilian sector after the model of the military establishment. A society is militaristic if its civilian members behave like soldiers, value discipline above freedom, pay more respect to valor than to work."

Distinctions between military and civilian life are being obliterated: The United States military establishment is modeled after the business corporation, and not conversely; generals behave like board chairmen, soldiers like clerks. As Morris Janowitz notes, within the military there has been a "shift or organizational authority from discipline based on domination, to organization control involving manipulation." The danger of war today grows out of the finely honed rationality of gamesmanship; it does not stem from what Bertrand Russell calls "the ferocious ... prejudices ... of the military-industrial fanatics."

Professional soldiers are seldom militant. The first requirement of military life is not belligerence but obedience. For an army to become a useful instrument of policy it must be stripped of fanaticism. As Hoffman Nickerson writes: "Professional soldiers are craftsmen ... you do not have to excite them by telling them their enemies are fiends." In the Thurmond hearings on troop indoctrination, General Shoup of the Marine Corps said that he did not want his men to "hate the enemy" because hate engendered (and depended upon) fear, which breeds defeatism and reduces fighting efficiency.

It is primarily in unstable societies that officer corps are insurrectionary; normally the military is content to follow and obey. In the United States, military presidents from Grant to Eisenhower have been mild and passive; they are usually less bellicose than our idealists. The General Walkers are atypical. Military men in foreign-policy positions have proved no more aggressive than civilians; in fact, says Walter Millis, they have often had to "hold back the sporadic and truculent impulses of political people and diplomats ..." The training of the professional soldier and the codes of military life create a rather cautious outlook.

But what of the industrialist? An erratic ferocity was

perhaps the dominant trait of early capitalism, of the Robber Barons. However, corporate capitalism today calls forth a different style of leadership—contrast McNamara with Henry Ford I. The managerial elite is now rarely fanatical and the psychopathic types are usually eliminated in the long climb up the organization pyramid. "The corporate manager today," writes A. A. Berle, "is essentially a civil servant ... There is common interest among corporation administrators in maintaining conditions permitting them to act with a minimum of control, and their enterprises to go on working; and there is a common desire for an orderly system in which they play a prominent part."

Monopoly has curtailed risk in capitalist enterprise and the rationalization of economic life has curbed "adventurism," in both business and politics. Like the medieval church, the primary aim of the modern corporation is continuity. Corporate capitalism engenders a confused conservatism, which if fatuous is not ferocious.

While big business may speak the muted rhetoric of the cold war, it still seems more interested in salesmanship than anticommunism. (The Chamber of Commerce and the head of the New York Stock Exchange backed the recent wheat deal with the Soviet Union and the president of the Chamber has called for trade with Red China.) Most large corporations have not supported the radical right. Fred Cook points out that leading defense contractors (Boeing, Lockheed, General Electric) have used rightist propaganda (Communism on the Map, writings by Fred Schwartz) for public relations purposes, and that an ex-General Motors president made a $300,000 contribution to the anti-communism school of Harding College in Arkansas. But when the big money has to go to

Arkansas to find an ideologist, the danger cannot be quite as grave as Cook suggests. Fifty years ago it could buy spokesmen at Harvard and Yale.

All established corporate structures are conservative, and regard the overly-zealous—the fanatic—as more disruptive than the dissenter. In the Middle Ages the church isolated its religious zealots in monasteries; today the Russian leadership has curtailed its reactionary Stalinists just as the American establishment has sought to control its Birchites. Big business "leans" to the right; big communism "leans" to the left; but probably both would accept a harmonious center position.

Both the Soviet and the American elite have advocated competitive or peaceful coexistence. Erich Fromm contends that while the Soviet elite uses the language of revolution it is, at bottom, concerned with the preservation of the communist establishment. A. A. Berle, the most articulate spokesman of corporate capitalism writes:

Assuming continued peace, in any long view the American and Soviet systems would seem to be converging rather than diverging so far as their organizational and many of their economic aspects are concerned ... (There is) no essential reason (why they cannot cooperate) provided cooperation is real and not an attempt to weaken the other, awaiting the movement of ultimate conflict.

Paradox II: The pressure for war comes from the public: Mass democracy generates a unique pressure for war: it fosters a climate of irresponsibility while it frustrates the urge for heroic action. The demagogue who cries for war usually finds a following, not because people are bloodthirsty, but because the call for valor and sacrifice elevates them above the dreary routines of peace. People have rather enthusiastically supported every war since the

Napoleonic period and there are many indications that men "enjoy" war; suicide rates decline, birth rates rise. During the war the economy runs in high gear, and confining social patterns are suspended. War is thus a liberating experience to those whose peacetime existence is devoid of excitement and challenge. Consequently, peace movements have never captured the popular imagination.

Immediately before World War I, radicals proclaimed that the conflict would be terminated through a general strike, should the oligarchy be foolish enough to launch a war. But as Norman Thomas once remarked, the war had been in motion scarcely a week before socialists were killing one another just as if they were Christians. In all countries, writes Raymond Aron, "(there was) an explosion of national fervor. Patriotism overrode social resentments and revolutionary aspirations." Since World War I, organized mass opposition to war has all but vanished. The peace issue has almost no appeal to the electorate. In the 1962 Congressional elections, none of the candidates who made peace a principle issue was elected to office, and those who ran as independents received a bare 1 percent of the primary vote.

For most men modern life requires a concentration on immediacies. Reflecting on public indifference to disarmament, Nathan Glazer writes: "People understand the possible dangers of atomic war well enough, but it appears a distant and abstract idea as against the immediate prospect of unemployment, relocation, retraining." The people live from day to day, elected officials from term to term; neither is disposed to take a long view of historical developments nor feels a stake in the remote future.

It might well be argued that the power elite, or the ruling class, has a more clearly defined "rational self-interest" in avoiding war than does the general public. It is not control by the elite but the absence of clear lines of authority which creates the greatest danger of war.

Paradox III: Increased military power reduces military security: In a world which is an amalgam of 1984 and Alice in Wonderland, not the least of the contradictions is the fact that any increase in weaponry reduces the security of everyone. It is disarmament and arms control, therefore, that become a "defense measure." Actually the concept of defense has been outmoded and current strategy is based on deterrence. But as Norman Cousins observes: "one nation's deterrence is another's incentive." The United States atomic monopoly did not prevent but stimulated Russian development of the bomb, and the success of Soviet rocketry was a prime incentive for our own missile program. The mutual possession of nuclear weapons with instant delivery systems, tends to nullify the value of possessing them. As Liddel-Hart writes, "the natural consequence of nuclear parity is nuclear nullity." The thermonuclear stalemate has now been given official recognition by Secretary of Defense McNamara:

> We are approaching an era when it will become increasingly improbable that either side could destroy a sufficiently large portion of the other's strategic force, either by surprise or otherwise, to preclude a devastating retaliatory blow.

With the thermonuclear stalemate and the dawning recognition that the "communist threat" is not primarily military, interest has turned to other forms of war. "The cold war," writes Robert Osgood, "is neither war nor peace in the orthodox sense, but a continuing struggle for power, waged by political, psychological and economic means as well as by a variety of military and semi-military means."

As the focus of conflict shifts from the organized world of nation-states to the grey chaos of colonial countries, conventional as well as nuclear arms are rendered useless. Attention has thus shifted to guerilla war which is a matter of politics, not arms. To succeed, guerilla operations must elicit the support of native populations. Confronted with revolutionary movements, the U. S. military apparatus has repeatedly proved impotent. It could do nothing about the "Cuban problem." And our military aid to South America, says Senator Wayne Morse, "is the most important cause in the deterioration of U.S.-Latin American relations." To this extent the military program has increased, not diminished, our military insecurity.

Strategists need to rethink the concept of "preventive war." Prevention is not preemption but the elimination of the sources of conflict. "Our problem," says George Kennan, "is no longer to prevent people from acquiring the ability to destroy us—it is too late for that. Our problem is to see that they do not have the will or the incentive to do it."

Paradox IV: The military program has undermined the garrison state: The revolution in warfare has destroyed the mass army and with it the psychological foundations of the garrison state. The war emotions of hate of the enemy induce the population to make the sacrifices needed to maintain the war machine. In 1948 the critics of universal military training saw in it the dreaded spectre of goose-stepping Nazis. But no one who has actually observed the college R.O.T.C. or the play-warring of the national guard (or regular Army) could see the program as the mother of the garrison state. Military service has been sold to both the public and the participants in terms of rational civilian values—upward mobility, adventure, sociability. There is hardly a mention of honor and patriotism, the values of classic militarism.

Since the time of Caesar the military has been an avenue of social ascent and, to that extent, a democratizing force. Today in America military service is often a way out and up for men from deprived groups—the Southern Negro, the slum boy. The 2.5 million men under arms probably have a more meaningful life than would otherwise be available to them. As civilians they would only swell the ranks of the unemployed by another 30 percent. Ideally, better use could be made of unemployable labor; but given the structure of American society a large army is perhaps the lesser of domestic evils. The results of universal military training have been benign, if not beneficial. Conventional forces today, like Roman legions, are primarily administrative rather than fighting organizations.

In addition the new machinery of war has called into being a class of technicians which bears no resemblance to military men of the past. In psychology and style of life, the military scientist or the engineer working on a missile or space assignment is no different from his colleagues in a university or a corporation. Moreover, the need for skilled specialists now enables the government to define education as a form of defense. Of the $700 million in financial aid directly to college students, $246 million comes from the federal government, and $100 million of that amount as "national defense scholarship loans." Over half of the "research and development" of the country is financed by the federal govenment ($5.6 billion in 1959), five-sixths of it directly through the defense department. But research and development is not inseparably linked to the war effort; it is a way in which the arms race could be formed into a space race without disrupting the economy. The new war technology has made disarmament economically feasible.

Mass war production has passed away with the mass army. Heavy industry areas—such as the Great Lakes region—are even now experiencing the economic impact of disarmament as defense-spending shifts to the east and west coasts. Even with record defense expenditures, unemployment increases and economic stagnation continues throughout much of the country.

When it is no longer possible for Senators and Congressmen to obtain defense contracts for their states, they may begin to look for other forms of government subsidy. "Economics," says Fred Cook, "has begun to throw its powerful arguments behind the idealistic and humanitarian pleas of those who are seeking to stop the arms race." Even so, it is virtually inconceivable that our vast military establishment would ever be dismantled. But it might be possible to turn the powers of the Pentagon to other purposes than destructive warfare.

Paradox V: The pentagon as an instrument of social reconstruction: Inherently our military establishment is neither reactionary nor progressive; it merely carries out the mandate of the state. Historically, armies have served mainly as a police force—from 1890 to 1917 strike-breaking was the main function of the U. S. Army, but in the 1950's the same organization was used to enforce school integration. The U. S. Army has also carried out valuable engineering projects: surveying and exploration in the early 19th century, flood control and dam building in the 1930's. Conceivably the Pentagon could become an institution for social and economic planning. It does have both the "know how" and the power to implement the vast changes which our society requires. There is no intrinsic reason why the power of the Pentagon cannot be used constructively in economic policy, education, urban renewal or even social welfare—both at home and abroad.

Even the military aid program has more constructive potentialities than is often realized. As colonial countries pass from tribal-feudalism to nationalism the native armies are expanded and become "instruments of modernization ... extending literacy and technological and administrative skills ... as well as building certain social overhead capital (sewer and transit systems, surveying, etc.) ... Burma, Turkey and Nasser's Egypt are cases in point." Unfortunately, most U. S. military aid goes to support reactionary and repressive regimes—Korea, Taiwan, and South Vietnam receive over half of all U. S. military aid to underdeveloped countries. But that is the result of a political, not a military decision. That the military can carry out a "democratizing program" was shown by MacArthur in Japan. In fact, the Pentagon could probably handle foreign aid more effectively than civilian agencies, since it has the power to resist local business and feudalistic pressures. For the same reasons it might also be used to cope with certain domestic problems such as urban renewal.

Paradox VI: The war emotions are potentially creative: The warfare state has superseded the welfare state, a generally lamented change. Yet if the basic meaning of war and welfare could be disentangled the former might appear the nobler cause. After 20 centuries of Christianity the concept of welfare still has little force. In western culture welfare comes as an afterthought, to be attended to only when the main business of life is settled. Singularly devoid of idealism and imagination, the welfare state was conceived and executed in the joyless spirit of the dole. Welfare, as understood and practiced in our time, makes the individual a passive recipient. Warfare, on the other hand, transforms the person into an active participant in a collective enterprise and thus evokes the altruism in men. As Gilbert Murray wrote in the aftermath of World War I:

"It is not that men want to kill, but they want to face death and peril. They want to put forth for one great moment the extreme effort of mind and body of which they are capable. They want to do it for others, for some great unspecified cause, so that if they live those whom they saved will adore them, and if they die multitudes will bless their memory."

Human society itself seems to have grown out of a union for common defense. "Only by the imperative need for combination in war" writes Herbert Spencer, "were primitive men led into cooperation." Robert Ardry contends that man himself descended from a now-extinct weapon-using ape. The machinery of war precedes the technology of agriculture and commerce, and all our evolution has not washed out the love of war.

The appeal of war is too profound to be neutralized by the sensible arguments of rational men. As William James noted half a century ago "the horrors make the fascination of war." Men need to prove to themselves and others that they are unafraid; they embrace the horror of war in order to conquer their own fears. When the peace movement points to the suicidal destructiveness of modern war, it provokes others to profess their willingness to die for civilization and thus demonstrate their bravery. "War is the province of danger," writes Clausewitz, "and therefore courage above all things is the first quality of the warrior ... war is the province of physical exertion and suffering ... war is the province of chance." Danger, courage, exertion, suffering, chance—the benefits of peace seem ignoble by comparison. That is why the search for peace will fail if peace is conceived as merely the absence of war.

"War," writes William James, "has been the only force that can discipline (i.e. integrate) a whole community, and until an equivalent discipline is organized, I believe that war must have its way." *The task is not to eliminate war but to change its object;* the task is to wage war against the natural enemies of all mankind, as President Kennedy said in his inaugural address. The "real enemy" is not totalitarian communism but the dehumanization of man which has resulted from the cataclysmic social upheaval of our time.

Can science be conceived as a battle for truth, or education as a war against ignorance? Science resembles war in many respects: it is a communal venture, with its strategy and tactics of inquiry, often involving bitter conflict between opposing camps but without bloodshed. And what is politics but the continuation of war, except by other means—to reverse the famous dictum of Clausewitz. Even military strategists are coming to see the cold war as a social and economic contest rather than a conflict of armed camps; it is thus that the character of war may be transformed from a destructive to a constructive activity.

March 1964

Does Military Deterrence Deter?

RAOUL NAROLL

In a time when Polaris submarines patrol the seas and Minuteman missiles are poised for flight at the flick of a switch, it sometimes seems as if modern military technology had created an entirely new, uniquely terrifying human situation in which past experience provides no answers to our present dilemma. How could such problems as the "balance of terror" or the credibility of the Strategic Air Command possibly be solved by considerations of military antiquities such as the fire-and-movement tactics of the Iroquois Indians or the exchanges of hostages among the Hottentots? But the waging of war goes back a long way in human culture. The techniques change, but the underlying human propensities for war—and for peace—remain constant.

It is known that primitive tribes—although lacking the destructive capability of civilized peoples—have a wider variety of military practices and warlike attitudes. A know-

27

ledge of how and why primitive peoples made war may shed light on the prospects for war or peace in our own time.

When we sort out all the arguments men make about war and peace—in UN debates, around the Geneva conference tables, in the editorial columns—most of them these days turn out to be variations on four basic theories about the causes and prevention of war:

- the arms race,
- deterrence,
- cultural exchange,
- cultural selectivity.

Each theme has its intellectual proponents who see it as the key to understanding the origins and solutions of the problem of war.

THE ARMS-RACE. This is a favorite theme for many academic authors, the Society of Friends, Ban-the-Bomb petitioners, and White House picketers of various descriptions. The theory holds, simply, that wars are caused by armaments. In an arms race each side strives without limit for military superiority. Neither can be satisfied with simple parity, because an underestimated rival may at any time achieve a technological breakthrough that will give *him* superiority. The psychological climate generated in an arms race is such that each side is likely to interpret the rival's capability as intent: "We are simply protecting ourselves in case of attack, but *they* are arming for war." An arms race thus becomes a circular, self-generating phenomenon of ever-increasing danger. To those who see the problem this way, there are only two possible alternatives—disarmament or annihilation.

DETERRENCE. This theme is most often used in current war/peace literature. Those who have faith in deterrence believe that military preparations can make for peace by vastly increasing the costs of war. A would-be aggressor, in a rational calculation of gain and loss, can be made to realize that the costs of warfare outweigh any possible gain. The advocates of deterrence point out that there is no defense against a nuclear war, and consequently our best hope is for a stable, credible deterrent. For a deterrent to be stable it must be invulnerable so that increased effort against it would be futile. Mutual invulnerability would, from this point of view, stabilize the arms race in a balance of terror. This balance would then, presumably, allow conflicts to shift to limited wars, and to an eventual stabilization and finally to reduction of war.

CULTURAL EXCHANGE. War is simply a large scale case of fear of strangers. Such prejudice against foreigners can be dispelled by first-hand contact, and when contacts increase, war becomes less likely. The exchange enthusiasts attempt to stimulate cultural exchange of every kind. Balletomanes can thank them for the visits of the Bolshoi and Kirov Ballets to these shores, and American actors and musicians can thank them for long-term engagements in the world-wide tours of *Porgy and Bess* sponsored by the State Department. Although such variants of cultural exchange are rather new in human experience, certain kinds of exchange—for example, hostages or wives—have been practiced between rivals for millenia.

CULTURAL SELECTIVITY. War is a basic factor in determining the rise and fall of civilizations. No human society exists alone; it lives with other societies and it must react to threats or be subjugated. Weaker peoples may be eliminated by stronger ones, or their social system radically altered. As societies react to the threats they pose to each other, those traits that make for success in warfare tend to outlast those that do not. This theme is sounded (in language not so anthropological) by those who see current international conflicts as a battle for survival between The American Way of Life and Russian and/or Chinese Communism.

Anthropological studies of primitive societies seem quite remote from such pressing questions of peace or war. What can comparisons of primitive military tactics or the tendency to trade women among Hottentots, Andamans, or Iroquois tell us about the invulnerability of hardened missile sites or military uses of space? While the special circumstances of our own generation, our own decade, this year and next, must obviously dominate the thinking of policy makers, an understanding of the direction in which the deeper currents run can help shape policies with a chance of success over the long term. Let us see what the findings of a cross cultural survey (see box, page 16)—examining the warfare patterns of primitive peoples all over the world—can contribute to the quest for peace in the 1960's.

The two major rival hypotheses about the relationship between armaments and warfare are the *arms race* hypothesis, and the *deterrence* hypothesis. The *deterrence* hypothesis holds that to preserve peace one must prepare for war; in other words, that an orientation to war in a society is inversely related to the frequency of its wars. The *arms race* hypothesis holds that preparation for war tends to make war more likely; thus an orientation to war is directly related to the frequency of war.

We tested these hypotheses by studying the selected cultures for several factors:

■ Warlike traits—such as the possession of guns—that seem to indicate an orientation toward warfare.

■ Frequency of warfare. We divided the cultures into two groups—those where warfare is frequent and those where it is not.

■ Correlations between each warlike trait and the frequency of war. If, for example, all forty-eight cultures in this study have guns, and if they all report frequent warfare, we have found a perfect positive correlation between guns and war. This means that (provided there are no errors in our data) whenever we find a society that has guns, we can predict without a qualm that it is plagued with frequent war. If all forty-eight societies should turn out to have guns and none of them report frequent war, we have found a perfect negative correlation. This means that whenever we encounter a society with guns we will be quite sure that it is rarely troubled by war. If all forty-eight units have guns, and half report frequent wars while the other half do not, then there is no correlation at all; finding that a society has guns won't tell us anything, one way or another, about the likelihood of war. The closer a correlation gets to being perfect the greater the likelihood that reasonable conjectures can be made about other societies possessing similar traits.

These are the warlike traits we finally selected as indications of a military orientation:

- use of fire-and-movement tactics;
- flexibility in the use of surprise tactics;
- multiple expectations of what could be gained by warfare;
- a large number of potential enemies;
- fortifications;
- military preparations other than fortifications;
- boundaries set along the lines of natural obstacles, such as rivers and mountain ranges;
- Western technology, including possession of guns or tools or an expressed interest in firearms;
- expressions of hostility (to test the Freudian theory that if hostility is not expressed within the culture, it will be turned outward in the form of aggression against others).

Some of these traits have subcategories, and nearly all

require some additional explanation.

FIRE-AND-MOVEMENT. According to Harry H. Turney-High's book, *Primitive Warfare: Its Practice and Concepts,* the tactic of first firing on the enemy from a distance and then moving in for hand-to-hand combat is a standard doctrine of modern civilized armies and a characteristic that distinguishes primitive from civilized tactics. The systematic use of fire-and-movement in attack requires a higher degree of coordination and control than the use of either projectiles or hand-to-hand combat alone. This kind of combat is more lethal than simpler tactics and warriors must be specially trained to fight this way. We assumed, then, that a group that uses this tactic is more strongly oriented to war than one that does not.

FLEXIBLE SURPRISE TACTICS. In modern warfare, surprise is a basic tactical principle; the attacker tries to strike his enemy unexpectedly whenever he can. However, surprise is not a universally applied military tactic. Some primitive tribes simply line up at extreme missile range and work up from hurling insults to hurling rocks at each other; this tournament-like war usually ends when the first enemy is killed. This kind of combat is a prearranged tryst, like duels under the European *code duello.* In other tribes, however, the warriors will not fight at all unless they can be sure of taking the enemy by surprise. Tribes like this usually send out raiding parties that lurk near the hostile settlements until they can catch their victims unaware. If the victims are alerted, the attackers simply go home.

The most militarily effective attitude toward surprise, of course, is to seek it but not to insist upon it. We held that societies who were capable of this flexible attitude toward surprise tactics had a stronger military orientation than those that held out for surprise alone or those who stuck to tournaments.

MULTIPLE EXPECTATIONS. An anthropologist, as an observer from the outside, probably cannot say with certainty what the causes of primitive warfare are. However, it is possible for him to make a much simpler and very useful set of observations about what the members of a war party in a particular culture have in mind when they set out for the attack. This "expectations" approach to primitive warfare was introduced by the anthropologist Quincy Wright in an earlier cross-cultural survey. Wright stated that military expectations in primitive tribes occurred in a certain order, such that the first expectation was always present in warfare; the second was never found without the first, nor the third without the other two, etc.

Our study, like Wright's, found that military expectations did occur in a certain order. The scale they formed ran this way:

1. Revenge and defense. Tribes fight to gain satisfaction for injuries (like murder or witchcraft spells), or to expel a foe from their territory. *All* warring tribes have this expectation.

2. Revenge, defense, and plunder. Tribes may also fight, in addition to the expectation above, for booty of some economic value—cattle, wives, slaves, land, cannibal victims (where the whole body, rather than some ceremonial portion, is consumed for food).

3. Revenge, defense, plunder, and prestige. In addition to both expectations above, warriors will go to battle to prove their military prowess—for instance, to acquire scalps or victims for ceremonial cannibalism.

4. Revenge, defense, plunder, prestige, and political control. The incorporation of the defeated enemy into the political system of the victor becomes an additional goal of warfare. Tribes where all of these expectations are in force, we assumed, are more likely to go to war than tribes where

only some of them occur.

MANY POTENTIAL ENEMIES. For each culture unit in the study, we tried to estimate the total number of war-making units which the society might consider to be potential enemies. If a society had more than ten potential enemies, it scored high on this measure; one with less than ten enemies scored low. As this measure actually worked out, the primary contrast was between societies with about five potential enemies and those with more than twenty-five. Our working hypothesis on this point is simply that the larger the number of potential foes, the more likely it is that there will be trouble with at least one of them.

MILITARY READINESS. Societies that carry out routine reconnaissance missions, or regularly post sentinels, or have a customary place for warriors to assemble in case of danger have this trait. We consider its presence an indication of a military orientation.

FORTIFICATIONS. Clearly, societies that build fortifications, like fences or man traps, have warfare in mind.

NATURAL OBSTACLES AS BOUNDARIES. We made the working hypothesis that societies that locate their boundaries along the lines of natural obstacles—like rivers or mountain ranges—were more concerned with the possibilities of warfare than societies that did not.

WESTERN TECHNOLOGY. The possession of guns, Western tools, and/or a lively interest in firearms were taken as indications of war orientation.

REPRESSED HOSTILITY. Societies can express their hostility through malicious gossip or quarreling or public ridicule or insults; a society in this study that did none of these things was considered to have a degree of repressed hostility which might find expression in warfare.

Once these traits of military orientation are defined, the next step in the process is to measure the frequency of war in each unit. Using the writings of ethnographers as sources, we considered warfare to be frequent when they used words like "perpetual," "periodic," "annually," "history of wars and conquests," to describe a culture's warfare involvement. Frequent warfare is absent where such reports say that war is "rare," "unusual," "sporadic," and so on. In the absence of more precise, comparable measurements, we were content to assume that the societies which had references to frequent wars fought more often and more intensively than the other societies.

Now we are ready to look for significant correlations. First let us see how the *frequency of war* is related to the characteristics of military orientation which we have defined.

The first conclusions that emerge clearly from these correlations have to do with deterrence. If the deterrence hypothesis were correct, then societies with strong military orientations would have less frequent war. *This study gives no support at all to the deterrence theory.* Very few of the measures of military orientation seem to have any impact, one way or the other, on the frequency of war. Strong negative correlations, which would support the deterrence hypothesis by demonstrating that war frequency decreases as military orientation increases, are completely absent.

The only significant correlations—*multiple expectations, military readiness, forts,* and *hostility*—are positive, and seem to indicate that these military orientations are positively associated with frequent wars. The strongest relationship that shows up is the positive correlation between *war frequency* and *military expectations.* Since that is so, let us also take a look at the relationships between *military expectations* and the other war-orientation traits:

Military Expectations Correlations

Trait	Strong Positive	Moderate Positive	No Relationship
Fire and movement		+	
Many enemies		+	
Military readiness	+		
Forts	+		
Boundaries			O
Technology			O
Hostility			O

Now let us see how the *frequency of war* is related to the characteristics of military orientation which we have defined:

War Frequency Correlations

Trait	Strong Positive	Moderate Positive	No Relationship
Fire and movement			O
Surprise sometimes			O
Multiple expectations	+		
Many enemies			O
Military readiness		+	
Forts		+	
Boundaries			O
Technology			O
Hostility		+	

The measures of warlike orientation most closely associated with *military expectations* seem to be *military readiness* and *fortifications*. That is to say, societies that expect more kinds of satisfactions from successful warfare tend to be societies which fight more frequently and which make more preparation for war. They also tend to be societies with large numbers of *potential enemies,* that use *fire-and-movement* tactics.

What we are saying, in other words, is that these data offer a kind of mild and tentative support for the arms race hypothesis. However, the positive correlations between war frequency and the two armaments measures—*readiness* and *forts*—are not very large, and they could possibly be a chance result. It is also possible that the existence of *military readiness* and *fortifications* are the *result,* and not the cause, of frequent warfare. The *arms race* remains a possible interpretation of this data, if we see all three variables—war frequency, military preparations, and fortifications—as reflections of an underlying war orientation.

We have subjected the notions of *deterrence* and the *arms race* to a cross cultural test; now let us examine the idea that the significance of warfare is its role as an agent of cultural survival.

No single factor plays the dominant role in the selection of traits in cultural evolution; we know that warfare is one of a number of possible trait-spreading mechanisms. The question that concerns us here is not whether warfare explains everything about cultural selection but whether it plays a part of any consequence at all in deciding which traits are retained and which are dropped. What we are asking here, in contemporary terms, is whether the "American Way of Life" or Communism is more likely to survive and possibly spread if the United States or the Soviet Union and/or China are militarily successful.

In this study we measure the effect of warfare on culture in terms of territorial change. There are a number of reasons for using this measure. If we had chosen to use "success" in warfare, we would have run into the difficulty of defining success in different ways for different cultures.

In some cultures, the pure emotional satisfaction of expressing hostility seems to be the chief object of war. In others, bringing home trophies is the standard. Modern societies, whose wars are fought by professional military men to gain ends defined by professional statesmen (who are usually military amateurs) define success in war in terms of imposing the will of the victorious nation (that is, the will of that nation's statesmen) upon the people of the defeated nation.

If we stick to territorial changes, our task is simpler. For all societies, defense of tribal territory when challenged is seen as a desirable outcome of war. The opposite possibility —the complete loss of tribal territory—can mean the complete extinction of the culture as a distinct way of life. This was the fate of such enemies of the Iroquois as the Neutrals and the Hurons, for example. In the course of recorded history, many highly influential, civilized cultures have perished utterly—their languages forgotten and their political organizations annihilated: this was the fate of the Sumerians, the ancient Egyptians, the Minoan Cretans, the Hittites.

This study indicates that territorial change is usually accomplished by force of arms. Of the fifty societies which we looked at for data on territorial change, twenty-one reportedly had no change during the period recorded (usually the century preceding colonial conquest). Of the twenty-nine that did have changes in territory, only three experienced the change peacefully (and one of these, the Araucanians, posed so great a military threat to its neighbors that one suspects that intimidation, rather than generosity, was responsible for its territorial accretions).

Territorial change, then, is a reasonable measure of the chances of survival of a culture, and such changes are almost always the result of warfare. We used two measures of territorial change: *growth* and *stability*. Both measures consider the ratio of territory the tribe gained or lost during the period studied to the territory the tribe had at the beginning of the period. The *growth* measure also takes into account the direction of the change—territory gained or lost.

The *growth* measure, by itself, would not be sufficient as a measure of cultural survival. The *stability* measure ignores the direction of change. Since territorial change almost always occurs through war, and since the outcome of a war is a very chancy matter, the society that keeps out of war as much as possible and avoids both gains and losses of territory may be the society most likely to survive.

The significant correlations between measures of war orientation, territorial growth, and territorial instability show several important relationships:

■ Territorial growth has a strong positive correlation with Western technology and a moderative positive correlation with military readiness.

■ Territorial instability has a strong positive correlation with military expectations and also a moderate positive correlation with military readiness.

Thus societies whose territories increase are characterized by Western technology and, to a lesser extent, military readiness. The most plausible explanation is that military preparedness tends to make for territorial expansion. The correlations also show a strong tie between territorial instability and military expectations. Societies which hope for a great deal from warfare are societies whose boundaries are likely to change, one way or another. It is tempting to explain this as a three-link chain of influence, with war frequency leading to increased expectations, and increased expectations leading to instability by making tribal land the stakes of warfare. The results here are equivocal, but they do demonstrate that warfare is an agent of cultural selectivity, and that the notion that we can best preserve our way of life by throwing away our arms is dangerously naive.

There is another naive theory of the causes and cures of warfare that is part of our present-day mythology: the theory that wars are simply a kind of prejudice against strangers, and that therefore we can prevent war by getting to know our enemies better. There are certain obvious difficulties with this proposition: in view of the profound value differences now existing between modern nations, it is quite possible that the better we get to know our enemies the more thoroughly we will dislike them. For the time being, however, we will put aside this possibility and subject the cultural exchange theory to our cross-cultural test.

We found useful data on three measures of peaceful intercourse between peoples: subsidies, trade, and women. A subsidy is a payment that one tribe makes to another for the single purpose of assuring a military alliance. When a weak society is paying out sums to a strong one, we think of the transaction as a tribute the weak people pay for the privilege of being left alone. Perhaps as often, however, the money is paid between nations of equal military strength (money flowed from 18th century England to her continental allies like Frederick the Great of Prussia), or from the strong to the weak (as rivers of foreign aid stream out from the US to her allies in the underdeveloped world). By trade we mean an exchange of goods of any kind—including slaves or wives—between potential enemies. Women—whether they are purchased, wooed, or raped—become part of their husband's household; the exchange of women, therefore, represents the most complete form of cultural contact. In many primitive groups men seek wives in communities which are also their potential military foes.

Our comparisons, regretably, show no significant relationships at all between the frequency of war and these three measures of peaceful intercourse.

Our survey of primitive tribes has yielded a number of results that are relevant to current US policy. The study indicates that in the very long run preparation for war does not make peace more likely. It does not seem to make much difference either way, but if it makes any difference at all it is in the direction of making war more likely than peace.

The study shows at the same time that military preparedness in the long run tends to favor territorial growth. Technological innovation seems to be especially effective. This finding supports the common-sense notion that you protect your culture by being prepared to defend it, and is quite incompatible with the position of the unilateral disarmers who claim that a country can best ward off attack by demonstrating its own peaceful intentions. Further study would be necessary to make the results on territorial growth more meaningful. It would be especially useful to identify several types of military preparedness which are substantially unrelated to each other. If territorial growth should prove related to each of these types, the preparedness hypothesis would be very strongly supported indeed.

The findings about military expectations do not have much bearing on current policy, simply because the military expectations of the rival powers today are at their maximum. This is to say that, if war occurs, there appears to be no limit to the kinds of benefits the victor might hope to derive. This is not to deny that both sides to a nuclear exchange might suffer losses far greater than any conceivable gain from victory, but only to state that if one side is clearly victorious in a general war it will not limit its demands upon the survivors of the defeated power.

The findings about peaceful intercourse indicate that it

is not realistic to hope that person-to-person programs will do much to ameliorate the international situation. There may well be other reasons amply justifying such exchanges, but this study can offer no support at all for the idea that they lessen the likelihood of war.

Clearly, more creative approaches to the way peace problems can be solved in the second half of the twentieth century are required if our culture, too, is not be become merely a reference point in a future study of warfare.

January/February 1966

Non·Govermental Organizations

LOUIS KRIESBERG

When the fourteenth World Ploughing Contest was held in Christchurch, New Zealand, in May contestants from every part of the globe arrived to take part. An equally diverse group assembled in Munich last July for the International Dairy Congress. Tokyo will be the scene of the World Road Congress later this year, and the British Paper and Board Makers' International Association of Paper Historians convened in the university town of Oxford in September. Doctors of many nationalities will gather in cities on every continent to discuss recent advances and obstacles in specialized fields of medical research.

Such international nongovernmental organizations (NGO's) now number almost 2,000, compared with fewer than 200 at the beginning of the century. They include groups with interests ranging from bicycling to nuclear physics.

The burgeoning of such organizations is due largely to

the increasing specialization of both work and leisure activities in industrialized societies. Aided by the increasing speed and decreasing cost of international travel and communication, people with special interests are crossing national boundaries more and more often to compare notes and promote common goals in groups such as the International Chamber of Commerce and the International Union of Health Education. With the exception of sharp drops preceding the two world wars and during the early 1950's, the rate of NGO formation has increased steadily.

NGO's may help ease world tensions. Perhaps they are even an index of the extent to which a world society already exists. They foster the development of international perspectives by reinforcing interests that cross-cut national boundaries. Their activities ameliorate the material and social conditions—the hunger, disease, and overcrowding—that underlie certain international conflicts. Formulas for settling international dissension may be developed in them and then incorporated into international law. They may even develop structural arrangements for handling conflicts among their own members that can later be used by governmental organizations such as the UN and its affiliates.

Most NGO's are concerned with occupational activities. Scientists the world over, for example, share interests in better crop yields and the conquest of crippling and killing diseases.

These like or common interests may spur them to joint efforts; and even their national differences may provide the basis for complementary interests and active exchange. But as members of different political systems, the members of various occupational and other kinds of organizations may also have some conflicting interests. This would seem especially likely between Americans and Soviets.

Can Americans and Soviets put aside their enmities to

promote, as members of the same voluntary organizations, common or complementary rather than conflicting interests? Is cooperation—a significant step beyond mere coexistence —really possible? A recent study I made of the nature and membership of NGO's suggests that it is.

About one-third of all NGO's restrict membership to some geographic area. Of the remaining, 21 percent have members from both the U.S. and U.S.S.R., 50 percent from the U.S. but not the U.S.S.R., 3 percent from the U.S.S.R. but not the U.S., and 26 percent from neither. If the generally high U.S. level of participation in NGO's and the very low Soviet level are considered, this means that the U.S. and U.S.S.R. are more likely to be in NGO's with each other than in NGO's in which the other is not represented.

The likelihood of joint membership varies further with the type of organization. NGO's which are made up of workers—for example, trade union organizations—are numerous, but there are few in which both the U.S. and the U.S.S.R. are represented. Such organizations constitute about 10 percent of the NGO's in which the U.S. but not the U.S.S.R. is represented, 14 percent of the ones in which the U.S.S.R. but not the U.S. participates, and 17 percent of the NGO's to which neither the U.S. nor the U.S.S.R. belongs; but they constitute only 1 percent of all the NGO's in which both nations participate. The pattern for NGO's in the area of commerce and industry is similar: 11, 4, 18, and 2 percent, respectively. On the other hand, in science and scientific research, the percentages are quite different: 4, 0, 2, and 18 percent, respectively.

NGO's may be classified in terms of their potential for consensus. The types are intended to reflect the varying degrees to which members of the international community, and particularly the U.S. and U.S.S.R., share goals and beliefs about the means to reach these goals.

■ Type 1 NGO's are concerned with technology, science, medicine, or sports. Consensus is presumably relatively high.

■ Type 2 consists of the social or economic NGO's organized by employer, profession, or trade union; they include groups in commerce and industry, social and political science, law and administration. In these, consensus is presumably moderate.

■ Type 3 includes NGO's dealing with matters about which consensus is presumably low—philosophy and religion, international relations, social welfare, education and youth, and the arts. The arts are included because officially recognized writing, painting, and film-making in the Soviet Union tend to be dominated by the aesthetic of "social realism," a highly idealized depiction of Soviet life that strongly promotes the Soviet ideology.

On the whole, the findings presented in Table I show that the U.S. and U.S.S.R. are most likely to be represented in organizations concerned with matters of presumably high consensus. About half of the NGO's in which they both participate are in the science-health category, while among the organizations in which neither participates, only about one-fifth are concerned with such matters.

In areas in which consensus is high, issues are often viewed as technical matters. Where consensus is low, value differences are likely to be prominent. But as a consideration of organizational structure will show, the extent to which an issue is viewed as a technical or a value matter is not inherent in the issue itself.

Even when Americans and Soviets find sufficient cause to become members of the same NGO's, some areas of conflict inevitably remain. How do organizations with such joint membership keep from being hamstrung by continual dissension? How do they carry out their day-to-day activities so as to minimize potential conflict?

The fact that these organizations often have higher levels of activity than those in which either or both the U.S. and the U.S.S.R. are absent is ample evidence that the former organizations, despite the risk of disruption, do function quite well. They are more likely than the latter to report engaging in activities such as coordinating research; providing services like libraries, abstracting services, and training programs for members; and developing standards or agreements about nomenclature and uniform codes.

The puzzling feature of the situation is that they do so without any relative increase in the size of the organizational staff which might seem necessary for carrying out these operations. This is because, with considerable personnel, the staff or an executive secretary often has relatively great power in the organization's policy formation. The delegation of such power to staff members is not likely to occur in an organization whose members have many conflicting interests—each side fears that the staff is in league with the other. It is not surprising, then, that NGO's with joint Soviet and American participation are somewhat less likely than others to have staffs of ten people or more.

Further decentralization of power in NGO's with joint U.S. and U.S.S.R. participation occurs due to the relative simplicity of organization—that is, the small number of organizational levels. The rank and file are not isolated from the decision-making core by an elaborate superstructure. However, even in the absence of such centralized decision-making, there are few general meetings in which the rank and file can participate directly in policy formation.

Taken together, these findings show some baffling inconsistencies. Joint U.S. and U.S.S.R. participation does not seem to lessen organizational activity, but the development of a large staff to implement this activity may be inhibited. Similarly, an elaborate number of organizational levels may be lacking; but frequent general membership meetings are not substituted to compensate for this structural arrangement. These inconsistencies are partially resolved when we consider one other organizational characteristic: the number of committees in the NGO's.

Despite the jokes about committees and their proliferation, they can be a useful device for organizations. They tend to transform problems from political issues to be decided by bargaining and negotiation to technical matters to be resolved by consensus among experts. Thus, the distinction between technical and nontechnical issues depends largely upon the persons trying to solve the issue and how they handle it, not on the issue itself or on the content area. If the mode of reaching a decision involves logrolling and bargaining and the style of the discussion is polemical debate, the issue will be nontechnical and political. Certain conditions can make such features more prominent. If the participants have clear constituencies who can hear the discussion, if there are many constituencies represented, and if the question is phrased in such broad terms that basic value differences are attached, then the issue is not likely to be viewed as a technical one.

Establishing committees can affect these conditions. Committees meet in relative privacy, and constituents do not hear the discussion. Members of a committee may be selected because of their specialized knowledge—their "expert" qualities; this makes it more likely that they will discuss the issue in technical terms and feel independent of definite constituencies. A small committee limits the number of constituencies involved. Handing problems to a committee usually means first dividing the problem into some of its components, and this makes each component seem relatively technical. And fundamentally, a few persons meeting regularly and frequently can develop rules of

TABLE I—TYPE OF NATIONAL PARTICIPATION IN NGO'S

Type of NGO	U.S. and U.S.S.R.	U.S., but not U.S.S.R.	U.S.S.R., but not U.S.	Neither U.S. nor U.S.S.R.
Science, health, etc.	53	22	18	18
Economic, social, etc.	28	41	43	56
Religion, art, international relations, etc.	19	36	39	26
Total	100	99	100	100

TABLE II—NUMBER OF NGO COMMITTEES BY TYPE OF NGO AND NATIONAL PARTICIPATION

Number of Committees	Science, health, etc.		Economic, social, etc.		Religion, art, international relations, etc.	
	U.S. and U.S.S.R.	Not U.S. and U.S.S.R.	U.S. and U.S.S.R.	Not U.S. and U.S.S.R.	U.S. and U.S.S.R.	Not U.S. and U.S.S.R.
None	52	75	47	64	50	69
1-6	14	5	9	10	11	8
7-10	7	1	4	4	3	2
11 or more	9	1	11	3	6	2
Some, but number not given	18	18	28	19	31	19

discussion and common understandings. The shared understandings diminish value differences.

The number of committees NGO's have is highly associated with whether or not the U.S. and the U.S.S.R. both participate in them. (See Table II) If the U.S. and U.S.S.R. both participate, the NGO is much more likely to have committees than if either or both parties are not represented. Of course, large NGO's tend to have more committees than small NGO's. But even holding the size factor constant, those with joint American-Soviet participation tend to have the most committees.

The use of committees, then, shows ways that organizations can be integrated along international lines and still maintain their activities somewhat independently of the amount of consensus or conflict among their members. It also shows that international give and take—for example, the sort of open exchange that can occur in frequent general membership meetings—must often be limited in order to assure the functioning survival of such organizations. These restraints circumscribe their role in fostering international contact, but NGO's can and do still serve as pilot projects for improving world cooperation.

December 1967

FURTHER READING SUGGESTED BY THE AUTHOR:

Preventing World III: Some Proposals edited by Quincy Wright, William M. Evan, and Morton Deutsch (New York: Simon and Schuster, 1962). See "Transnational Forums for Peace" by Evan, a discussion of ways NGO's contribute to international peace.

International Non-Governmental Organizations by Lyman C. White (New Brunswick, N.J.: Rutgers University Press, 1951). Descriptions of membership in and activities of a variety of important NGO's.

Soviet Sport by Henry W. Morton (New York: Collier Books, 1963). The history of sports activities in the U.S.S.R. and changes in its participation in international events.

The International Labor Movement by Lewis L. Lorwin (New York: Harper and Bros., 1953). The history of changing relations among trade-union organizations of the U.S.S.R., the United States, and the rest of the world.

Yearbook of International Organizations (Brussels, Belgium, Union of International Associations, 1966–67 edition). A comprehensive dictionary of all existing, incipient, and deceased international governmental and nongovernmental organizations, together with information about activities, structure, membership, address, and officers.

Comments on
Report from Iron Mountain

In August of 1963, if we can believe Leonard C. Lewin, a Special Study Group was set up, under Government auspices and with melodramatic secrecy, in order

1. to determine what problems the United States would face if permanent peace broke out; and

2. to draw up a program to deal with these problems.

The Study Group's sponsor was probably an *ad hoc* Government committee at, or near, the cabinet level. Included among the Group's 15 members were an economist, a sociologist, a cultural anthropologist, a psychologist and a psychiatrist, and one literary critic. The 15 met once a month, usually for two days, over a period of two and a half years, the first and final meetings being held in an underground nuclear shelter inside Iron Mountain, in upstate New York (near war-gamer Herman Kahn's Hudson Institute). A report was unanimously agreed upon, then submitted to the Government "interagency committee," along with an urgent recommendation that its contents be kept secret.

There the matter rested—until winter 1966, when a member of the Study Group, "John Doe," came to New York, looked up Leonard Lewin, and handed him a copy of the report, explaining that while he himself accepted all of the *Report*'s conclusions, he also strongly believed that its findings should be made public. Lewin promptly found a publisher, wrote an introduction, included an interview with John Doe, and refused to say another word about the report's origins.

Report from Iron Mountain on the Possibility and Desirability of Peace, with Introductory Material by Leonard C. Lewin (The Dial Press, New York, 1967) says, in essence, that while permanent peace may be possible, it probably would not be desirable. To quote the *Report*: "It is uncertain, at this time, whether peace will ever be possible. It is far more questionable, by the objective standard of continued social survival rather than that of emotional pacifism, that it would be desirable even if it were demonstrably attainable."

Peace, the *Report* concludes, is hell. If society is to remain stable, wars must continue. "War itself is the basic social system, within which other secondary modes of social organization conflict or conspire." The indispensable functions that war and war preparedness serve are assigned to various categories, perhaps the key ones being economic, political, sociological, and ecological.

1. *Economic.* Military spending, by virtue of its independence from the normal supply-demand economy, acts as a balance wheel. "It is, and has been, the

essential economic stabilizer of modern societies."
Among possible substitutes offered are a comprehensive
social-welfare program; a fantastically elaborate dis-
armament-inspection system; and an even more enormous investment in space research. Social-welfare programs, however, would not, in the long run, eat up
enough resources, and in addition would not remain
very long outside the normal economy. A disarmament-
inspection system would also not prove "wasteful"
enough, and would be incongruous in a world permanently at peace. Space-research programs, the *Report*
decides, appear to be the only realistic substitute. (It is
the *only* substitute the Study Group warmly endorses.)

2. *Political*. It is only because of the threat of war
that individual nations, and stable governments, can
exist. ". . . 'war' is virtually synonymous with nation-
hood. The elimination of war implies the inevitable
elimination of national sovereignty and the traditional
nation-state." Furthermore, military spending serves
to keep a certain portion of the population poor, thus
maintaining "necessary class distinctions" and a ready
supply of unskilled labor. As a possible substitute, new
external enemies might be created—like invaders from
outer space, "fictitious alternate enemies," or air and
water pollution (which would have to be deliberately
intensified). According to the *Report,* only the creation
of "fictitious alternate enemies" offers any promise.

3. *Sociological*. The army and the draft serve to re-
move antisocial members from society. War itself
catharsizes aggressive impulses. And the existence of an
external menace induces citizens to become patriotic
and subservient to the state. "Allegiance requires a
cause; a cause requires an enemy." Possible substitutes:
programs like the Peace Corps; "Socially oriented blood

games"; and "A modern, sophisticated form of slavery." Of the substitutes, only slavery, the *Report* concludes, may prove "efficient" and "flexible."

4. *Ecological.* War has been the chief evolutionary mechanism for maintaining a proper balance between the population and the supplies the population needs to survive. Here, at least, war has a drawback: It is not eugenic. Nuclear wars, for example, kill off the superior as well as the inferior. A possible substitute *and* improvement: ". . . a universal requirement that procreation be limited to the products of artificial insemination," along with "A comprehensive program of applied eugenics."

What the *Report* does, then, is to legitimize war. The Special Study Group's key conclusion is: "If it were necessary at this moment to opt irrevocably for the retention or dissolution of the war system, common prudence would dictate the former course."

The bulk of the available evidence suggests that the book is a hoax. As for the perpetrator, nominees have included Richard Rovere, John Kenneth Galbraith (who told *Trans-action,* archly, "If I had been a member of the Study Group, I would have been sworn to secrecy"), Kenneth Boulding (whose *Disarmament and the Economy* is quoted), Vance Bourjaily, and—anticlimax of anticlimaxes—Leonard Lewin. All roads, however, lead to Leonard Lewin: he is a freelance journalist who has reviewed a book on think-tanks, he edited *A Treasury of Political Humor,* and he loaned a working draft of the *Report* to a *Trans-action* informant.

The *Report* is far from being "just a hoax," though, and it cannot be dismissed out of hand. Despite its many specious arguments and its spotty knowledge of social science, it is also an acutely accurate satire. What it satirizes is explained by John Doe: ". . . what they wanted from us was a different kind of *thinking*. It was a matter of approach. Herman Kahn calls it 'Byzantine' —no agonizing over cultural and religious values. It is the kind of thinking that Rand and the Hudson Institute and [the Institute for Defense Analysis] brought into *war* planning. . . ." War-gaming has become peace-gaming.

The fact is that the *Report* could have been compiled entirely from authentic sources. There are many social scientists doing this kind of investigation; there are members of the Defense Department who think like this. As one reader has observed, "This provides a better rationale of the U.S. Government's posture today than the Government's official spokesmen have provided. A better title for the book, in fact, would have been the same as Norman Mailer's novel: *Why Are We in Vietnam?*"

The threat that the *Report* holds is not so much that it will be believed and acted upon, but that it *has* been believed and acted upon. Significantly, *Trans-action* has found that those readers who take the book seriously tend to be Government officials. Upon inquiry, sources very close to the White House were authorized to say that the files and libraries of the Executive Office of the President have been reviewed, and although some reports in the general subject area covered by the *Report* were found, there was no record of this particular report. These sources believed, therefore, that no comment was appropriate at this time. Informally, they observed that their statement does not rule out the possibility that the *Report* was sponsored either in the White House, by some Congressional committee, or by some other agency within the Federal Establishment.

More important than the need to know whether *Report from Iron Mountain* is authentic or not, the public needs to know what the current thinking of U.S. Government agencies is in regard to (1) what problems the United States would face in the event of peace and disarmament and (2) what programs should be devised to deal with these problems.

One Defense Department informant has admitted that some of his colleagues have agreed with the *Report*'s conclusion that the Vietnam war is sound because at least it helps preserve stability at home. Another informant, who works at the highest levels in strategic planning within the Pentagon, asserted after reading the *Report* that he saw no reason to consider it a hoax, since he often comes upon reports that read in much the same way. Yet a third person—a recent alumnus of the defense Establishment—found the *Report* quite credible. All this testifies to the enormous gap between secret Governmental assessments of questions of war and peace, of disarmament, and of the "war system" and official public stances—as much as it testifies to Mr. Lewin's skill as a creator of social-science fiction.

The publication of *Report from Iron Mountain*, whatever its source, should become an occasion for a new public demand for a penetrating examination and evaluation of Government reports on strategic planning for disarmament and peace. The extent to which a belief in the desirability and inevitability of "the war system" is built into the operational conceptions of the Government is of deepest public concern, not to be thwarted by claims that these are matters of state that require secrecy.

Irving Louis Horowitz

HENRY S. ROWEN

The most interesting aspect of the *Report* is the reaction to it in the press and among reviewers. It has been described as "original," "acute," "skillful," "chilling," "genuine." It is none of these. It is superficial and lacking in bite. That it should create a certain commotion is, perhaps, more a reflection on the generally low level of public discussion on matters of strategy, international affairs, and disarmament than anything else.

The consequences of disarmament or, to use the terminology of the *Report,* the abandonment of the "war-system" is certainly a subject worthy of serious discussion. So it is conceivably worthy of satire. After all, the U.S. Government supports the objective of general and complete disarmament. If that state of affairs, however it might be defined, were to be brought about, it would certainly be associated with a profound change in relations among states and even within them. And given the variety of opinions to be found in our society, there may be some people who hold a position resembling that presented in the *Report*. Evidently some reviewers think so. But for most of the arguments put forward in the *Report,* I can find little substance in fact, nor can I identify the advocates of the view held.

Statements such as "An economy as advanced and complex as our own requires the planned average annual destruction of not less than 10 percent of gross national product . . . ," or "As an economic substitute for war [a social program] is inadequate because it would be far too cheap," or "the rate of pollution could be increased . . ." in order to have an enemy to fight, or the suggestion that slavery be reintroduced to our society in order to maintain social control, are not ludicrous versions of serious views; they are merely ludicrous.

Most of the *Report* deals with the social and economic effects within the nation state of general and complete disarmament. The *Report* has little to say about the international consequences of disarmament. Here it has largely overlooked what those who "commissioned" the *Report* might have expected as an essential topic for discussion. It is characteristic of the casual nature of this work that it fails to cite Tom Schelling's original and important observations on the consequences of "total" disarmament and to deal with the issues he raises. (Thomas C. Schelling, "The Role of Deterrence in Total Disarmament," *Foreign Affairs,* April 1962.)

Finally, the *Report* would have a greater effect if it had more of the marks of a genuine, Establishment-commissioned product. The little things—concessions, references to contemporary international affairs, hedges, touching of the bureaucratic bases—are largely missing.

ANATOL RAPOPORT

The consensus among reviewers is that *Report from Iron Mountain* is a hoax. But how can one tell the hoax from the real thing these days? There are, of course, the give-aways, the thinly veiled satirical allusions; but what if these were deleted? Satire makes a point if certain aspects of the situation satirized are magnified to grotesqueness. Thus *Doctor Strangelove* was a satire, because there the life of the planet depended upon the availability of 55 cents to put into a pay telephone. But what is there in the *Report* that stretches credibility?

Recall that when *On Thermonuclear War* first came out, the late James R. Newman refused to believe in its authenticity. Now we know better. The barrier of the Unthinkable has been breached once and for all.

Well, not quite. It has been breached on one side only and remains as solid as ever on the other. If the valiant souls who dare look into the abyss were really daring, they would find charming solutions for some of the most tantalizing problems that they pose.

Take one of the principal theses of the *Report,* namely that the continued existence of war or, at least, of the war machine is essential to the health of an advanced economy and to the integrity of a society. Grant the thesis. Now what is wrong with this solution: All war production continues and even expands, as the needs of the economy demand; but the products are declared obsolete immediately instead of in two or three years, which is presently the case? Consequently the products are destroyed as quickly as they are produced. Not only is employment not curtailed but it is actually expanded by the added demolition personnel. Also storage space is saved.

It may be objected that this procedure amounts to disarmament. However, as long as we are in the realm of the Unthinkable, let us pursue the implications, as befits rational beings. Let us not chicken out. Objections to disarmament are of two sorts, namely the obvious ones, derived from conventional wisdom, and the sophisticated ones, outlined in the *Report*. Now the latter have been disposed of by the proposed solution. Disarmament can be accomplished with full war production undisturbed. As for the other objections, these too can be met.

Why not agree with our potential enemies to exchange military and strategic personnel, each side to do with the personnel so delivered as they see fit? This may be formally equivalent to having each side extend its disarmament to include software as well as hardware, and is therefore subject to the same objections as hardware disarmament. Psychologically, however, the procedure has altogether different overtones. Each side *increases* its security by having the military leadership of the other at its mercy. Thus the mutual distrust and hostility can persist and even grow. The ideological war (necessary, according to the *Report,* to hold society together) can flourish. The military personnel of each side (now hostages) can be subjected to intensive interrogation or can be depleted by a controlled liquidation program. In fact, the whole game of escalation and deterrence can be played on this level.

Here, then, is a program that gives us the opportunity of avoiding the unpleasant by-products of *both* peace *and* war. The constructive and creative aspects of war can go on unimpeded. (Indeed, the reduction of the lag of obsoleteness to zero will stimulate an even more rapid development of war technology.) Nations need not become soft and decadent. The strategists can continue to plot each other's countries' destruction to their hearts' content. Disarmament does not jeopardize the safety of the disarmed nations, since in return for disarmament each gets a chance to deplete the military personnel of its enemies (it need not trust them to do it). The aggressive impulses of man can find an ample outlet on the hostages.

That such proposals were not incorporated in the *Report* speaks for its authenticity.

*   *   *

JESSIE BERNARD

Before commenting on this report, I would like to correct one erroneous rumor. On page XXII, Doe states that "there were no women in the Group." It so happens that I was a member. But my contributions were so contrary to the tenor of the discussions—one blew a fuse when fed into a computer, and computer time was a major expense of the project—that, by consensus, it seemed best for me to drop out. As Doe notes, some of the sessions were rough; we got on one another's nerves. But they wanted a unanimous report, and they ended with no important differences.

I had taken them at their word, namely that they wanted to tackle "the relevance of peace and war . . . to . . . sociological relationships . . . , to psychological motivations, to ecological processes. . . ." But they kept rejecting my suggestions. They wanted to talk about "the antisocial elements," unemployment, social-welfare programs, cultural uplift; I wanted also to talk about the relations between the sexes.

In one session, for example, I pointed out war's emancipating effects on women. I reminded them of the liberating results for women of the Punic Wars, which—taking men away—gave women a great deal of experience in the administration of enterprises. I reminded them that World War I had been followed by the first sexual revolution of this century; women achieved the right to demand orgasm and they also achieved the right to smoke and cut their hair. World War II opened up to women a wide gamut of jobs never before available to them. War, in this sense, was a great plus for women.

But since this point had zero-sum aspects (the war

gains for women often having a minus aspect for men), the Group was reluctant to feed any of it into the computer. They gave as their excuse that they were uncertain as to whether they should feed it in as a cost or as a benefit to the system as a whole.

Finally an answer was provided by Hill, the psychiatrist. War was clearly a plus for men too, for although anything that upgraded women was clearly a cost to the men (he saw all relations between the sexes as zero-sum in nature, in conformity with so much exchange-theory currently fashionable), there was another angle. There were few things, he reminded us, if any, now left exclusively to men. There were even movements afoot to deprive men of the right to buy guns freely. Take war away from them and what did they have left? A line had to be drawn somewhere. The perpetuation of the war system was therefore clearly a benefit to the men, even if it did also incidentally help women.

This was acceptable to the Group until, after a bit of mulling, I reminded them that technology is increasingly depriving men of their monopoly on the war game. As we move more and more in the direction of a push-button war, women can take over quite nicely. Women can sit in the underground war chambers and monitor hostile flights and flying objects as well as men. They can push buttons as easily as men. They can steer unmanned rockets as well as men. In the future, all the really good wars will probably be turned over to women, leaving only the dirty little jungle wars to the men. In the prestigious wars, technology is making it as easy for women to displace men in the war game as in civilian industry. The day might even come, as the President said recently, when there will be a female chief of staff. The very thought of the war system under the control of women was just too much. . . . The horrors of war began to look as intolerable as the horrors of peace. That did it. My presence was so clearly abrasive that I withdrew.

Enough of this. War and peace are too serious to be left to the satirist. Especially to a satirist *manqué* like Doe, who is neither a Swift nor a Veblen nor even a Buchwald. There is not enough bite, not enough sublety, not enough outrage. He strives for wit but achieves only dullness. As a high-level researcher's *revanche* for Congress' ukase of some years back forbidding the inclusion of a "surrender" option in any defense research, it is fairly successful. As a *reductio ad absurdum* of the systems approach, it passes. As a spoof of the sociological functional tradition of the 1950s, which traced the function of every aspect of social systems (crime, ignorance, prejudice, corruption—the list is almost endless), it is a good try. But as the vehicle for "a serious and challenging effort to define an enormous problem" (xv), it is not nearly good enough.

The great overriding point he has is epitomized in the newspaper report, "Wall Street was shaken yesterday by news of an apparent peace feeler from North Vietnam. . . ." Although this may be viewed as only a modern variant and updating of the old Nye investigation of munitions-makers, there is a new angle that is crucial, namely that the "munitions-makers" have now become the great military-industrial complex that President Eisenhower warned us about. A large segment of the economy depends on the military-industrial complex. Peace, in fact, does threaten it, and many of our own perquisites along with it.

I fault the author's judgment in using the anonymity dodge. Instead of focusing discussion on the points he is trying to make, this posture will deflect it to the question of whodunit. A trivial question in comparison with the question he raises: Is war, as we have always thought, a tool of social systems or, as this book concludes, are social systems the tools of wars?

MARC PILISUK

There are several cogent issues raised by *Report from Iron Mountain*. Among them, the question of whether or not the enterprise is a satirical hoax (and I tend to favor this view) seems to matter least.

The fact is that the enterprise is distinctly reminiscent of the style, procedures, and tone of the new operations-oriented, free-wheeling brainstormers whose product is sold and solicited in policy circles as serious social-science analysis. In fact, the *Report* recalls these brainstormers with sufficient vividness to make us quake with fear about the process that does go on.

The early sections deal with the composition of the Special Study Group, and its indoctrination to answer the question set forth without bias. The method previews one that may soon be improved upon, as follows: Add 250 hours of behavioral-scientist time to seven full-time hardware types, one ex-intelligence man, one international-relations type with government experience, two successful industrialists, a regional planner, an eminent physicist, and a Negro (even if the last, because of the demand, must be rented from Hertz). To promote frankness, lubricate the group with some unspeakable jokes or rudeness. In the first section of the final report, insist that one has cornered the market on objectivity and has been able to transgress, in all subsequent conclusions, the moral sensibilities that hinder other mortals. The technique will eventually be amended to include abbreviated T-group (sensitivity-training) sessions, and will then claim that the participants will thereby have achieved either the equivalent of a psychoanalysis or, at least, the Dhyana of the ancient Buddhists. This emphasis upon gaining a virtual monopoly on truth by the purity of the group's cathartic expurgation, or by its own surprise when it saw the light, is something that distinguishes the possessed individual or group from the skeptical scientist or philosopher. The latter, however forceful about their current beliefs, remain dubious about the ultimate validity of these beliefs.

Because the technique is simple and because it disdains the hard work of the social scientist is not sufficient reason to reject the *Report*'s conclusions. With reference to finding an alternative to war, most serious social-science research, as the *Report* suggests, has been trivial—if not in its relevance or in the validity of its conclusions, at least in the paucity of its attempts to find an adequate answer to the question of why its research is not being put to use. Moreover, since empirical research requires some operational statement of what one is talking about, and studies come easier where the topic is limited in scope, few social scientists ever devote themselves to prolonged analysis of how or why the social system *as a whole* evolves into war or peace. Some serious scholars have written about the economics of disarmament (usually with the conclusion that it is manageable, given a pattern of resource reallocations and planning that is about as impossible as disarmament itself). Psychiatrists, anthropologists, and ethologists have written about aggression and violent war (usually with the conclusion that in man, at least, bloodless forms of hostile behavior and of resolving disputes may be possible). Other social scientists have produced a host of ingenious solutions—international armies, agencies, exchanges, alliances, friendships, detection techniques, and so on—all of which have been explored separately. But it is rare to find anyone brash enough to take on the whole gamut of questions at once. In this, *Report from Iron Mountain* stands out. It covers a broad expanse; refers with some familiarity to relevant literature in several fields; and creates hypothetical projections with the gusto of a first-year student in urban architecture creating a city.

The *Report* contributes some penetrating insights into the system of the think-tank operation. One is the use of consensual validation among like-minded people to replace evidence. "It was hard to figure out who were the liberals and who were the conservatives, or who were hawks and who were doves." Shown here are the limits of American pluralism as a check on military-industrial power. Real power determines not who wins out among various political protagonists, but who decides the smorgasbord of which protagonists or which issues will be considered. A currently circulating definition of a dove is: One who favors the least escalation. If pluralism is to operate, it requires something more than this as a counterpower to military interests.

A second insight into the think tank is the use of computer programs to resolve problems for which gross assumptions must be made (and then forgotten) so that the product can have a ring of scientific jargon that sounds good, or at least incomprehensibly authoritative, when presented in Congressional testimony or in special White House reports. Here the gem is the "peace games" method, described as a computer language with a superior capacity to interrelate data with no apparent common points of reference. The product of this method is illustrated with great poignancy in a footnote that explains the prediction that science could still continue to progress for two more decades after the end of the war system:

"This rather optimistic estimate was derived by plotting a three-dimensional distribution of three arbitrarily defined variables: the macro-structural, relating to the extension of knowledge beyond the capacity of conscious experience; the organic, dealing with the manifestations of terrestrial life as inherently comprehensible; and the infra-particular, covering the conceptual requirements of natural phenomena. Values were assigned to the known and unknown in each parameter, tested against data from earlier chronologies, and modified heuristically until predictable correlations reached a useful level of accuracy. 'Two decades' means, in this case, 20.6 years, with a standard deviation of only 1.8 years. (An incidental finding, not pursued to the same degree of accuracy, suggests a greatly accelerated resolution of issues in the biological sciences after 1972.)"

A third characteristic of the think-tank approach is a willingness to promote the causes of some morally-handicapped diviner of the future of mankind. The strategic framework, unhampered by sentiment, assumes that Machiavellian motivation and violence are not only real, but necessary for the best interests of society. If they lead to a destruction of most of society, so be it: The realist faces this prospect and looks beyond. Just as Herman Kahn can deduce the promising opportunities available in the post-nuclear-attack era, so does *Report from Iron Mountain* speak about the population-control advantages of nuclear weapons. Formerly, wars hurt the species by selectively killing off the strongest of its members. The species is now, fortunately, in for a better deal, according to the *Report,* since nuclear weapons will kill indiscriminately. Of course, the *Report* indicates that this gain in the gene pool may be offset by some genetic damage to the survivors (just as Herman Kahn notes, in *On Escalation,* that a nuclear exchange may produce casualties). But at least the stability of our social system would not be jeopardized by disarmament, withdrawal, idealism, or refusal to play the strategic game.

Behind all this satire, the book contains a provocative analysis of how dependent this country is upon war for the centralized planning and domination of resources and personnel that keep the society from embarking upon radical departures from its traditions. That this central argument is shored up by some apparently unfounded assumptions regarding the significance of killing to the culture, arts, science, and even the existence of social systems does not make the argument less valid. Two years ago I did some research into the military-industrial complex and came to an essentially similar conclusion, namely that American society, as we now know it, could *not* make the accommodations necessary to achieve disarmament reallocations, to achieve assistance of the type needed to avert extensive violence stemming from underdevelopment, or to achieve international jurisdiction of disputes.

If the conclusion that current American society is incompatible with peace is valid, the recommendations one makes still depend upon values. *Report from Iron Mountain* remains true to its asserted heritage of the assumed source of all great values, the war system, and it concludes that peace is not to be obtained or desired. Perhaps the recommendation is prophetic for, beneath the rationalizations and moralisms, American policy does continue to make the choices that make future violent conflict inevitable. Still, there are those among us who follow Jeffersonian values and would recommend instead that it is the American system, rather than peace, that has grown dangerous and unresponsive to our needs. Perhaps the United States, rather than peace, is the appropriate target for revolutionary restructuring. The *Report* is one attempt to hasten this process through exposure.

There is danger as well as promise in such satire. During the fallout-shelter controversy, a brilliant piece appeared in *New University Thought* entitled "On Serving Your Fellow Man." It dealt with the problems of convincing people of the advantages of (and overcoming their aversions to) orderly cannibalism in the food-depleted shelter. The approach ranged from the problem of ethics (serving the greatest number with the fewest number) to the problems of appetite (better recipes and prestige-advertising inducements). It was, unfortunately, no more absurd in its rationale than any other part of the shelter program. But I shuddered at the time to think that some secret Special Study Group —imbued with dedication and freed from emotional or moral compunctions—might pick up the suggestion and immediately engage in the technical problem of how to promote this new dimension in shelter living.

We have come a long way when the existing think tanks can plan for levels of genocide matter of factly and with only an occasional need even for secrecy. The *Report* stirs revulsion only in those who play the game in which people count. For the strategy theorists, and that may by now include too many of us, I fear that they have just picked up a trick or two that they might otherwise have missed.

I have been asked twice now whether I wrote the book. I did not. Anatol Rapoport, Kenneth Boulding, Noam Chomsky, Paul Goodman, Donald Michael, Amitai Etzioni, and Irving Horowitz are candidates whose wit, competence, and devotion to peace make them suspect. My great hope, however dim, is that it was done by some dropout from the RAND Corporation as an overture to his reentry into the family of man. My great fear is that the strategic framework of thought is so prevalent and so compatible with the competitive advantage of an affluent society that the *Report* describes a process of controlling the future that is too far along for warnings to be of value.

KENNETH E. BOULDING

I have been publicly accused of writing this book. I did not write it, and I knew nothing about it until I received a page proof, somewhat indirectly, from the publisher. Furthermore, I regard the suggestion that I wrote it as very close to being an insult. If the book is intended as a satire, as it may be, it is written with too straight a face to be wholly convincing. If it is "straight," it represents a point of view that I reject on both intellectual and moral grounds.

Intellectually, the work is clever pinchbeck, operating at the level of popularized folk science. Its economics is folk economics, in spite of the fact that it quotes *Disarmament and the Economy.* The author, or authors, of the work do not understand the significance of economic models and completely underestimate the flexibility of the American economy and its adjustability to any level of military or governmental expenditure.

The basic intellectual fallacy of the book, however, goes far deeper than its particular misunderstandings. It might be called the "functional fallacy." This is the fallacy of supposing that because something exists there must be a good reason for it. Thus, the world-war industry, as I have called it, exists at a certain level, say approximately 10 percent of the gross world product. There must be a reason for this, the book argues, and if the world-war industry were done away with, something specific would have to take its place.

This crude functionalism neglects what is the most important characteristic of social systems—that they operate on a loose dynamic with strong random elements and many degrees of freedom, and that their properties at any one time are simply the result of these loose dynamic processes up to that date. In other words, many things exist for which there are no good reasons at all, but simply because the dynamics of the system produce them. More specifically, many things exist for which there are no good reasons in human welfare, and the world-war industry is one of them. It exists because of a perverse dynamic and it can be done away with by changing the dynamics of the system.

Morally, the work, if "straight," is highly sinister. It is an attempted justification and legitimation of the war industry, and especially of the American war industry, at a moment when the institution of war is threatened with delegitimation because of its outrageously negative payoffs. What is attempted here is a legitimation of the military system, not in the ancient terms of courage and drama that have so largely been drained out of it, thanks to air power and the mass murder of civilians, but in terms of "peace" imposed by universal terror and oppression.

I console myself, however, with the reflection that the dynamics of legitimacy are very complex and that sophisticated attempts to create legitimacy frequently backfire. I am frankly interested in delegitimizing the war industry, and in spite of the fact that I suspect this document had the opposite intention, it may well turn out that its effect will be to further this delegitimization. The reaction may well be, "If this is how the war industry has to be justified, there must be something even more wrong with it than we think." In its results, therefore, this book may turn out to be on the side of the angels.

MURRAY WEIDENBAUM

From the newspaper articles alone, I could not figure out why Mr. Lewin modestly wished to cloak his work in semi-anonymity. A reading of the volume clears up that question rapidly. If this string of unsupported assertions and social-science fiction had been offered under his own name, it would have been laughed off the market as the malevolent musings of an uninformed crackpot.

I particularly regret seeing the numerous factual and analytical errors included in the sections dealing with economics. The general reader is likely to be hard put to separate fact from fiction. For example, "The Special Study Group" repeats the tiresome Marxian cliché that the Vietnam war was stepped up in 1965 "in the usual coordination . . . with dangerously rising unemployment rates." How should the general reader be expected to know that the truth of the matter was just the opposite? Unemployment rates—and total unemployment—were falling all through 1965 *prior* to the Vietnam buildup during the middle of the year. The unemployment rate was 5.2 percent in 1964. It declined from 5.0 percent in February 1965 to 4.5 percent in July 1965. It is hard to believe that such basic distortion of the truth is not malevolent.

Perhaps a more fundamental flaw is the author's contention that the economic and fiscal tools of Federal budget policy would not be effective enough to facilitate the shift of resources from military to civilian uses. The discussion here (page 21) is particularly illogical. First the reader is told that fiscal tools "can provide new incentives in the economy." In the very next sentence, the author states that these tools "reflect the economy; they do not motivate it." (My colleagues in sociology tell me that the sociological sections of *Iron Mountain* are poor, but that the economics chapter seems to be convincing. I will leave to the psychologists the analysis of how to con academics via "interdisciplinary" research.)

Any student of Economics 1 knows that government purchases of goods and services are indeed a source of "final" demand, that the Federal Government's buying of tables or chairs or post-office buildings or space satellites motivates private production and employment just as directly as private customers do. Witness the substantial shift of resources from civilian output to meet the needs of the Vietnam war.

Incidentally, this large and rapid shift of resources also belies the alleged geographical "inflexibility" of military production. The step-up in the Vietnam war has resulted in major shifts in the geographic, industrial, and occupational distribution of military purchasing in the American economy. While some Midwestern states have seen their military contracts double during the last few years, during the same period several of the far Western states—Washington, Utah, and Colorado—have had their defense orders virtually cut in half.

The industrial shifts in military demand during the last few years have been equally dramatic and belie the author's statement that "rigid specialization . . . characterizes modern war production." While the large aerospace and electronics firms have been obtaining declining shares of the military market, clothing and textile orders are up 240 percent, automotive vehicles are up 80 percent, and food is up 60 percent. Details are contained in *Economy Effect of Vietnam Spending,* Joint Economic Committee (Washington, G.P.O., 1967, 2 vols.).

Perhaps the greatest disservice that *Iron Mountain* renders is to lower the level of argument in the crucial dialogue on the prospects for peace. Until now the debates have centered mainly on different interpretations of a common factual basis. We are now reduced to the lower-level chore of cleaning up Lewin's literary litter before it pollutes the intellectual environment. Under the circumstances, it is unfortunate that *Iron Mountain* is receiving greater academic attention than its spiritual ancestor, that earlier anonymous and allegedly suppressed committee report, the *Protocols of the Elders of Zion.*

LEONARD J. DUHL

Whether this book is a hoax or not is irrelevant. What is important is the fact that it exists, and that it reflects a particular style of thinking.

Report from Iron Mountain serves a useful function in pointing out that a peacetime society needs new kinds of social planning to deal with the special problems created by peace. But the book points out this need with that type of long-range thinking that treats ecological models—models that incorporate demographic and geographic variables as well as sociological ones—as completely closed, almost fully controllable, rigid systems.

Irving Louis Horowitz has suggested that fascists use ecology as a model because it gives them their excuse for massive control—for control not just of matters we usually consider the legitimate concerns of government, but of matters (such as who will have children and who will not) that democratic systems consider the business of their individual citizens. An ecological model need not serve such fascistic ends, however. Treated as an open system, an ecological model for social planning can actually help ensure the survival of democratic procedures during the critical adjustments that our society will have to undergo, now and in the future, in order to adapt itself to a state of peace.

The essential fault of the *Report* is its failure to recognize (1) that planning from an ecological model, whether for war or peace, is a *process*—rather than the establishment of a set of rigid systems, and (2) that this process is not oriented toward stability, but toward change.

Our economic, sociological, ecological, cultural, and scientific concerns are concerns for those processes that permit change to occur in each system. The overall social system we seek to preserve is not what the *Report* calls "the survival of the social system we know today." Nor is it based solely upon a set of institutions for which "substitute" institutions must be created. Rather, it is a fluid system composed of changing institutions and processes through which we seek to enable every individual to control and affect the events that control his life.

If one views the problem of peace as an issue we must face, as the *Report* does, one must then give high priority to domestic concerns. And these concerns extend beyond the static and negative one defined by the *Report* as "the survival of social systems we know today." They are, instead, the development of new social systems—and modifications of existing ones—to permit the kind of domestic processes that will enable us to solve our internal problems without turning into a fascistic, controlled, or militaristic state. They require changes toward improvement, rather than merely viewing the stability of society as the "one bedrock value that cannot be avoided."

Certainly the two poles may be anarchy and control. But the planning procedures needed to ensure that our peacetime social system is between these two poles are not those that maximize the value of stability, but those concerned with creating mechanisms to guarantee that the values we hold dear to our society are maintained. How to create these mechanisms so that we can further human development, achieve health, and maximize citizen participation in those events that affect our lives—these are the important questions to which all else must be directed. And these are the questions that the *Report* fails to ask.

A peacetime society in which these mechanisms exist may not be perfectly stable and free of tensions. But social tensions are not war. Society can prepare itself for the tensions accompanying the negotiations for change that permit a society to be viable and active.

That social scientists would permit themselves to become party to a fascistic goal, as they have if this *Report* is real, truly requires that they reexamine their goals for our society. Years ago Kurt Lewin, in *Resolving Social Conflicts* (Harper & Row, 1948), said:

"it seems to be crucial for the problems of social science that the practitioner understand that through social science and only through it can he hope to gain the power necessary to do a good job. Unfortunately, there is nothing in social law and social research which will force the practitioner towards good. Science gives more freedom and power to both the doctor and the murderer, to democracy and Fascism. The social scientist should recognize his responsibility also in respect to this."

Report from Iron Mountain illustrates that the social scientist must reexamine any tendencies he has to define what is good as what is static and structured. It reveals how an ecological model can be twisted into a highly institutionalized and status-quo-oriented approach that negates the essence of ecology—change, and the participation of all segments of a system in the processes through which that change occurs.

BRUCE M. RUSSETT

That some people have accepted Leonard Lewin's cover story for *Report from Iron Mountain* illustrates how easy any government's job really is much of the time—some people will believe *anything*. It also illustrates once again the risks of satire. Ridicule often fails because some people have no sense of the ridiculous. To this reader at least, it is apparent that the *Report* is a spoof, if not on the whole a very funny one. It has to be a spoof simply because it is presented as the product of a handsomely-supported team that took a broad, general, long-term look at the most basic problems of American foreign policy. Anyone who knows our leaders also knows how small a government audience such a report would have. Virtually every official is totally immersed in day-to-day problems, though perhaps an occasional Nostradamus is assigned the task of maintaining a six-month horizon.

That some people have taken the *Report* at face value makes me worry even more than usually about the quality of the American debate on foreign policy. Much of its humor is black, with the best morsels reserved for the footnotes. My preferred tidbits are the allegedly-computerized projections based on the "peace games" computer language, replete with high orders of precision in probability levels, means, and standard deviations, all derived from "arbitrarily defined variables" where "values were assigned to the known and unknown in each parameter." Anyone who doesn't know that this is a put-on is a very sad victim of two-culture isolation.

But of course the truly sad part is that so very many people cannot recognize put-ons, as is evidenced by the only slightly more subtle hoaxes perpetrated in many real prognostications. Too many studies have used complicated procedures to "analyze" material that was little more than arbitrary assumptions rather than data. Similarly, the *Report* is a spoof of documents that state complicated conclusions about social reality as simple assertions, buttressed only by supreme confidence and an illustrative aside about the organization of the Inca empire. This sort of thing requires me to affirm, varying a famous question and answer, that there is *not* a John Doe.

Other victims of the satire, besides the hardnosed "strategic thinkers," are the peaceniks who have not understood the system they are trying to transform. Here the author(s) of the *Report* rise(s) above the style of gay potshots to warn us of the intractability of the war system—for me, one of the book's two serious purposes is to suggest just how hard it would indeed be to institute permanent peace. Those who would abolish war must examine their own unsupported assumptions, and do a kind of careful, massive, detailed research job that has never been attempted, and for which we have little more than the fraudulent substitutes parodied by this book.

Finally, the book seems to be most centrally concerned with the consultants and officials who "avoid" value judgments in their rigorous pursuit of deduction to objective conclusions unhindered by bias. In fact, the values of the putative authors are pervasive—stability is their highest goal. They are unwilling to take any risks to change the system or to revise the functions that the system serves; they seek survival without caring *what* survives. This unconcern with the *purpose* of America by those who guide its policies is the tragedy of our country and our profession. Perhaps it is because this syndrome is so familiar that so many readers did not recognize the put-on.

January/February 1968

Social Science Yogis
and Military Commissars

IRVING LOUIS HOROWITZ

"The bonds between the government and the universities are . . . an arrangement of convenience, providing the government with politically usable knowledge and the university with badly needed funds." The speaker of these words, Senator J. William Fulbright, went on to warn that such alliances may endanger the universities, may bring about "the surrender of independence, the neglect of teaching, and the distortion of scholarship." Many other distinguished Americans are worried by the growing number of alliances between the military and the university.

Instead of the expected disclaimers and denials from university officials, however, in recent months these men—from both the administrative and academic sides—have rushed to take up any slack in doing secret research on campus, asking that the number of projects they are already handling be increased. Arwin A. Dougal, assistant director of the Pentagon's office for research and engineering, has indicated that while some major universities are gravely concerned about academic research for military ends, most universities realize how important "classified research" is to the national security. Indeed, Dougal has said that many professors involved in secret research actually try to retain their security clearances when their projects are completed. Rather than disengaging themselves, they, like many university leaders, are eager to participate to an even greater extent.

Symptomatic of the ever-tightening bond between the military and the social scientist is a "confidential," 53-page document entitled *Report of the Panel on Defense Social and Behavioral Sciences.* It was the offspring of a summer 1967 meeting in Williamstown, Mass., of members of the Defense Science Board of the National Academy of Sciences. This board is the highest-ranking science advisory group of the Defense Department. The meeting's purpose: to discuss which social-science research could be of most use to the Department of Defense (DoD).

The Report of the Panel on Defense Social and Behavioral Sciences throws a good deal of light on current relations between the national government and the social sciences. Unlike Project Camelot, the abortive academic-military project to investigate counterinsurgency potentials in the Third World, this Report was not inspired by government contractual requests. It is the work of leading social scientists who have been closely connected with federal research. Unlike *Report from Iron Mountain,* this Report can hardly be described as a humanistic hoax. The authors are known, the purpose of the Report explicit, and the consequences clearly appreciated by all concerned. What we have in this Report is a collective statement by eminent social scientists, a statement that can easily be read as the ominous conversion of social science into a service industry of the Pentagon.

Most of the scholars who prepared this Report have one striking similarity—they have powerful and simultaneous academic and government linkages. They move casually and easily from university to federal affiliation—and back again to the university.

The panel's chairman, S. Rains Wallace, the exception, is president of the American Institutes of Research, a non-profit organization that does research under contract for government agencies, including the DoD.

Gene M. Lyons, who is executive secretary of the Advisory Committee on Government Programs in the Behavioral Sciences of the National Research Council (affiliated with the National Academy of Sciences), is also a professor at Dartmouth College. (He maintains, however, that he attended only one day of the meeting, and as an observer only.)

Peter Dorner, functioning through the Executive Office of the President on the Council of Economic Advisers, is also a professor of economics at the Land Tenure Center of the University of Wisconsin.

Eugene Webb, listed as a professor at Stanford University is now serving a term as a member of the Institute for Defense Analysis, specifically, its science and technology division.

Other panel members—Harold Guetzkow of Northwestern University; Michael Pearce of the RAND Corporation; anthropologist A. Kimball Romney of Harvard University; and Roger Russell, formerly of Indiana University and now Vice-Chancellor for Academic Affairs at the University of California (Irvine)—also shift back and forth between the polity and the academy. It is plain, then, that these men have penetrated the political world more deeply than members of past project-dominated research activities.

In addition to this similarity, nearly all of these social

scientists have had overseas experience, and are intimately connected with federal use of social science for foreign-area research. Yet, as in the case of Camelot, this common experience does not seem to produce any strong ideological unanimity. The men range from relatively conservative political theorists to avowed pacifists. This underscores the fact that patriotism and professional purpose tend to supersede the political viewpoints or credos these men may adhere to.

The Report closely follows the memorandum that John S. Foster Jr., director of Defense Research and Engineering of the Department of Defense, issued to the chairman of the panel. Foster's marching orders to the panel members requested that they consider basically four topics: "high-payoff" areas in research and development—"areas of social and behavioral science research in which it would be reasonable to expect great payoffs over the next three to ten years"; research to solve manpower problems; Project THEMIS, a DoD project for upgrading the scientific and engineering capabilities of various academic institutions so they can do better research for the Defense Department; and, finally, broad-ranging government-university relationships.

Before commenting on the Report, let me provide a summary of its findings and recommendations.

To begin with, the Report urges increased effort and funding for research on manpower, in all its aspects; for research on organization studies; for research on decision-making; for increasing the understanding of problems in foreign areas; and for research on man and his physical environment.

• Under "Manpower," we read, among other things:

"In order to make full use of the opportunities provided by Project 100,000 [to make soldiers out of rehabilitated juvenile delinquents] both for the military and for the national economy, we recommend that fully adequate funds be invested to cover all aspects of the military and subsequent civilian experience of the individuals involved."

- Under "Organization Studies":

"Research on style of leadership and improved methods of training for leadership should be revitalized."

- Under "Decision-Making":

"Techniques for the improvement of items which might assist in forecasting alliances, neutralities, hostile activities, etc., and for use in tactical decision-making need to be expanded, applied, and tested in the real world."

- Under "Understanding of Operational Problems in Foreign Areas":

"Despite the difficulties attendant upon research in foreign areas, it must be explicitly recognized that the missions of the DoD cannot be successfully performed in the absence of information on (a) sociocultural patterns in various areas including beliefs, values, motivations, etc.; (b) the social organization of troops, including political, religious, and economic; (c) the effect of change and innovation upon sociocultural patterns and sociocultural organization of groups; (d) study and evaluation of action programs initiated by United States or foreign agencies in underdeveloped countries.

"Solid, precise, comparative, and current empirical data developed in a programmatic rather than diffuse and opportunistic fashion are urgently needed for many areas of the world. This goal should be pursued by: (a) multi-disciplinary research teams; (b) series of field studies in relevant countries; (c) strong representation of quantitative and analytic skills; (d) a broad empirical data base."

- Under "Man and His Physical Environment":
"Continuing and additional research are needed on the effect of special physical and psychological environments upon performance and on possibilities for the enhancement of performance through a better understanding of man's sensory and motor output mechanisms, the development of artificial systems which will aid performance, and the search for drugs or foods which may enhance it."

- Under "Methodology":
"We recommend increased emphasis upon research in behavioral-science methodology. While this is basic to all of the areas listed above, it needs to be recognized as worthy of investment in its own right. The systematic observation of the many quasi-experimental situations which occur in everyday military activities must be made possible if we are to learn from experience. We recommend that a capability be established in one or more suitable in-house laboratories to address the question of how the logistical problems of such observation can be solved."

- On government-university relations:
"There is disagreement concerning the involvement of first-rate academic groups in behavioral science research relevant to long-term DoD needs. The task statement implies that DoD has not been successful in enlisting the interest and service of an eminent group of behavioral scientists in most of the areas relevant to it. This panel does not concur. We therefore recommend that the [National Academy of Sciences] Panel on Behavioral and Social Sciences be asked to address this problem and to determine whether, in fact, an acceptable proportion of first-rate academic workers are involved in DoD behavioral-science research."

"More high-quality scientists could probably be interested in DoD problems if DoD would more frequently state its research needs in terms which are meaningful to the investigator rather than to the military. . . . Publicity concerning the distinguished behavioral scientists who have long-term commitments to the DoD should be disseminated as a way of reassuring younger scientists and improving our research image."

Why did these distinguished social scientists accept the assignment from the DoD? Most of them seemed particularly intrigued by the chance to address important issues. They view the work done by the DoD in such areas as racially segregated housing, or the rehabilitation of juvenile delinquents through military participation, as fascinating illustrations of how social science can settle social issues. It is curious how this thirst for the application of social science led the panelists to ignore the prima facie fact that the DoD is in the defense business, and that therefore it inevitably tends to assign high priority to military potential and effectiveness. Further, the question of what is important is continually linked to matters of relevance to the DoD. In this way, the question of professional autonomy is transformed into one of patriotic responsibility.

In general, the idealism of social scientists participating in DoD-sponsored research stems from their profound belief in the rectifiability of federal shortcomings, as well as in the perfectability of society through the use of social science. Despite the obviousness of the point, what these social scientists forget is that the federal government as well as its agencies is limited by historical and geopolitical circumstances. It is committed to managing cumbersome, overgrown committees and data-gathering agencies. It is committed to a status quo merely for the sake of rational functioning. It can only tinker with innovating ideas. Thus federal agencies will limit investigation simply to what is immediately useful not out of choice, but from necessity.

The social scientist often imagines he is a policy formulator, an innovating designer. Because of the cumbersome operations of government, he will be frustrated in realizing this self-image and be reduced to one more instrumental agent. His designing mentality, his strain toward perfecting, will appear unrealistic in the light of what he can do. He gets caught up in theory-less applications to immediacy, surrenders the value of confronting men with an image of what *can be,* and simply accepts what others declare *must be.* Thus, what the social scientist knows comes down to what the Defense Department under present circumstances can use.

Although the initiative for this Report came from the social scientists, the DoD provided the structure and direction of its content. To a remarkable degree, the study group accepted DoD premises.

For example, the two major assumptions that influenced its thinking are stated baldly. First, since the DoD's job now embraces new responsibilities, its proper role becomes as much to wage "peacefare" as warfare. Peacefare is spelled out as pacification of total populations, as well as a role in the ideological battle between East and West. Toward such ends, it is maintained, social science can play a vital part.

Nowhere in the document is the possibility considered that the DoD ought not to be in many of these activities—that perhaps the division of labor has placed too great an emphasis upon this one agency of government at the expense of all others. Nor is it anywhere made clear that similar types of educational and antipoverty programs the DoD is engaged in are already under way in other branches of government—that DoD activities might be duplicating and needlessly multiplying the efforts of the Department of Health, Education and Welfare or the National Science Foundation.

The second explicit assumption the group makes is that hardware alone will not win modern wars; manpower is needed, too. Here the panelists see social science as providing data on the dynamics of cultural change and a framework for the needs and attitudes of other people.

But here, too, there is a remarkable absence of any consideration of the sort of "manpower" deployed in foreign environments; or of the differing responses of overseas peoples to such manpower. The foreign role of the U.S. Defense Department is simply taken as a given, a datum to be exploited for the display of social science information. In this sense, United States difficulties with foreign military activities can be interpreted as a mere misunderstanding of the nature of a problem. Expertise and objectivity can then be called upon where a policy design is lacking or failing. Thus even the DoD can mask policy shortcomings behind the fact of a previously inadequate supply of data. In this way, the credibility gap gets converted into a mechanical informational gap. Which is exactly what is done in the Report. All efforts, in other words, are bent to maximizing social science participation rather than to minimizing international conflict.

Still a third assumption of the panel participants—one that is not acknowledged—is that their professional autonomy will not be seriously jeopardized by the very fact of their dependence upon the DoD. Indeed, many scholars seem to have abandoned their primary research interests for the secondary ones that can be funded. And the main responsibility for this shift lies not with the DoD but with the social-science professions and the scholarly community at large.

As one panel member ironically noted, in response to my questionnaire, the position of the DoD is an unhappy reflection of university demands that individual scholars and university presidents pay for expanding university overhead and enlarge graduate programs—rather than any insistence by federal agencies that the nature of social science be transformed. Another panel member indicated that, whatever dishonor may exist in the present relationships between social science and the DoD, the main charge would have to be leveled at the professoriat, rather than at the funding agencies. And while this assignment of priorities in terms of who is responsible for the present era of ill will and mistrust can be easily overdone, and lead to a form of higher apologetics in which there is mutual accusation by the social scientists and government policy-makers, it does seem clear that the simplistic idea that the evil government corrupts the good social scientist is not only an exaggeration but, more often, a deliberate misrepresentation.

Reexamining the specific findings of first section of the Report, "High Payoff Research in Development Areas," leaves no doubt that the panelists mean by "high payoff" those potential rewards to be netted by the DoD, rather than advantages to be gained by social scientists. This is made explicit in the section on "Manpower," in which the main issues are contended to concern problems of improving the performance of soldiers equipped with high-level technology. It is in this connection that the panelists heartily approve of Project 100,000. Although (with the exception of two panelists) there is a special cloudiness as to the nature of Project 100,000, the panelists have no doubt that the employment of delinquents in this fashion makes the best use of marginal manpower for a "tremendous payoff" for the future efficiency of the defense establishment.

A number of the Report's recommendations amount to

little more than the repetition of basic organizational shib-
boleths. But even at this level, special problems seem to
arise. There is confusion in the minds of the panelists, or
at least throughout the Report that they prepared, about
what constitutes internal DoD functions as opposed to
those belonging to general military functions. The phrase
"military establishment" functions as an umbrella disguising
this ambiguity. Not only is the relationship between a
civilian-led DoD and a "military establishment" unresolved,
but beyond that the panelists appear willing to discount
the organizational intermingling of the DoD with other
governmental agencies—such as the Census Bureau, the
Department of Labor, and the Department of Health, Education, and Welfare.

This leads to a tacit acceptance of DoD organizational
colonialism. Not only is the DoD urged to be on the
lookout for other agencies' collecting similar data and doing
similar sorts of analyses, but also an explicit request that
the DoD exert a special effort to use the work of outside
agencies is included. On behalf of "cooperation," there
exists the risk of invasion of privacy, and other dangers
encountered when any single department functions as a
total system incorporating the findings of other subunits.

The Report contends that those parts of the armed services responsible for developing basic knowledge about
decision-making have done their work well. It is interesting
that no examples are given. Moreover, the military and
civilian personnel who provide support for decision-making
within the military establishment are said to have a rare
opportunity to contribute to this steadily improving use
of sound decision-making models for areas like material
procurement for frontline battle medical services. Nothing
is said about the nature of the conflict to be resolved, or the
values employed in such decisions.

While several members of the panel, in response to the questionnaire of mine, indicated that they held this Report to be an indirect resolution of problems raised by Project Camelot, the formulations used in this Report are similar to those used in the Camelot study concerning overseas research.

The Report states: "Comparative organizational work should not be done only within civilian groups such as large-scale building and construction consortia and world-wide airlines systems, but also within foreign military establishments." In Project Camelot, the same desire for military information was paramount. Curiously, no attention is given to whether, in fact, this is a high-payoff research area; or if it is, how this work is to be done without threatening the sovereignty of other nations. In other words, although the Report superficially is dedicated to the principle of maximum use of social science, this principle is not brought into play at the critical point. The ambiguities and doubts raised by previous DoD incursions into the area of foreign social research remain intact and are in no way even partially resolved.

The panelists are dedicated to the principle of high-payoff research, but appear to be disquietingly convinced that this is equivalent to whatever the members of the panel themselves are doing, or whatever their professional specialties are. Thus a high-payoff research area becomes the study of isolation upon individual and group behavior; or the area of simulation of field experiences that the military may encounter; or the study of behavior under conditions of ionizing radiation. It is not incidental that in each instance the panelists themselves have been largely engaged in such kinds of work. One is left with the distinct impression that a larger number of panelists would have yielded only a larger number of "high-payoff" areas, rather than an integrated framework of needs. This leads to a general suspicion that the Report is much more self-serving than a simple review of its propositions indicates.

The references to methodology again raise the specter of Camelot, since it is evident that no general methodology is demonstrated in the Report itself and no genuine innovations are formulated for future methodological directions. There is no discussion of the kind of methodology likely to yield meaningful prediction. Instead, the DoD is simply notified of the correctness of its own biases. We are told that "predictive indicators of a conflict or revolutionary overthrow are examples of the type of data which can gain from control applications." No illustrations of the success of such predictors is given. The purpose turns out to be not so much prediction as control of revolutionary outbreaks. This, then, constitutes the core methodological message of the Report.

As for Project THEMIS, designed to upgrade scientific and engineering performances at colleges and universities for the benefit of the Defense Department, the project titles at the institutions already selected do not furnish enough information to assess the actual nature of the research. A proposal of more than $1.1 million for research into "chemical compounds containing highly electro-negative elements" was turned down by the dean of faculties at Portland State College. Said he: "I know what the proposal was talking about. It could very easily be interpreted as a proposal involving biological warfare. The proposal could be construed as committing the university to biological warfare."

Among the universities now contracted for Project THEMIS work is the University of Utah, with the project title "Chemistry of Combustion." Newspaper accounts during the summer of 1967 indicated clearly that this project

was aimed at improving missile fuels. Additional illustrations could be given, but the point is clear: Project THEMIS
is what it claims to be, a program to involve universities
in research useful to the Defense Department.

The panelists assure us that "DoD has been singularly
successful at enlisting the interest and services of an eminent
group of behavioral scientists in most of the areas relevant
to it." They go on to say that, indeed, "the management
of behavioral science research in the military department
should be complimented for long-term success in building
the image of DoD as a good and challenging environment
in which to do both basic and applied research." No names
are cited to indicate that there are eminent clusters of
behavioral scientists working in the DoD. Nor is there an
indication whether "the eminent men" connected with DoD
are in fact remotely connected as part-time consultants (like
the panelists themselves) or intimately connected with basic
work for the government. And even though Foster's letter
indicates that there is a problem of recruitment and government-university relations, the panel simply dismisses this
as insignificant. Yet members go on to note that the DoD
image is perhaps more tarnished than they would like to
think; that, for example, the Civil Service Commission dis-
criminates against the behavioral scientist with respect to
appointments, and that it is hard to persuade behavioral
scientists that the DoD provides a supportive environment
for them. Despite the censure of the Civil Service Commission, it is claimed that the DoD has not been as attractive and as successful in social-science recruitment as we
were earlier led to believe.

More damaging, perhaps, is the allegation of the panelists that quality control of research at universities is not in
any way superior to that exercised within other research
sources such as the DoD. They tend to see "quality control"

as something unrelated to university autonomy and its implications for objectivity. Lest there be any ambiguity on this point, they go on to indicate in an extraordinary series of unsupported allegations that the difficulty is not one of social-science autonomy versus the political requirements of any agency of government, but rather one of bad public relations—which is in turn mostly blamed on "Representatives of Civilian Professional Organizations" who lack a clear picture of DoD requirements and yet testify before Congressional committees, which in turn are backed up by social and behavioral scientists who regard such DoD activities as a threat to academic freedom and scientific integrity, and who "are usually ignorant of the work actually being performed under DoD's aegis."

The specific committee hearings referred to are nowhere indicated. Certainly, the various hearings on such proposed measures as a national social science foundation, or on social accounting, do exhibit the highest amount of professional integrity and concern. It might be that DoD intellectuals are concerned precisely over the nonpolicy research features of such proposed legislation.

Finally, the panelists offer a gentle slap on the wrist to defense research managers who allegedly lack the time to address themselves to these kinds of problems. In short and in sum, the Report ignores questions having to do with social science autonomy as if these were products of misperceptions to be resolved by good will and better public relations between the DoD and the Academy. That such conclusions should be reached by a set of panelists, half of whom are highly placed in academic life, indicates the degree to which closing the gap between the academy and the polity has paradoxically broken down the political capabilities of social science by weakening its autonomous basis.

The panelists have enough firmness of mind to make two

unsolicited comments. But the nature of the comments reveals the flabbiness that results from the tendency of social scientists to conceive of their sciences as service activities rather than as scientific activities. They urge, first, that more work be done in the area of potential high-payoff fields of investigation that might have been overlooked in their own Report, given the short time they had available in preparing it. They further urge the establishment of a continuous group with time to examine other areas in greater depth and to discuss them more deliberately, so that high-payoff areas can be teased out and presented for cost considerations. In other words, the unsolicited comments suggest mechanisms for improving these kinds of recommendations and making them permanent. They do not consider whether the nature of social science requirements might be unfit for the bureaucratic specifications of Foster's originating letter.

In some ways, the very tension between social scientists and policy-makers provided each group with a reality test against which basic ideas could be formulated about policy issues. But the very demand for a coalescence of the two, whether in the name of "significant" research or as a straight patriotic obligation, has the effect of corrupting social science and impoverishing policy options.

The question that the Report raises with terrible forcefulness is not so much about the relationship between pure and applied research, but about what the character of application is to be. Applied research is clearly here to stay and is probably the most forceful, singular novel element in American social science in contrast to its European background. What is at stake, however, is a highly refined concept of application that removes theoretical considerations of the character and balance of social forces and private interests from the purview of application. The design of the future replaces the analysis of the present in our "new utopian" world.

The panelists simply do not entertain the possibility that the social world is a behavioral "field"' in which decisions have to be made between political goals no less than means. Reports cannot "depoliticalize" social action to such an extent that consequences do not follow and implicit choices are not favored. Innovation without a political goal simply assumes that operations leading to a change from one state to another are a value. The Report does not raise, much less favor, significant political changes in the operations of the DoD; and its innovative efforts are circumscribed to improving rather than to changing. However, efficiency is a limited use of applicability because it assumes rather than tests the adequacy of the social system.

The era of good feelings between the federal government and social science, which characterized the period between the outbreak of World War II and extended through the assassination of President John F. Kennedy, no longer exists. In its place seems to be the era of tight money. The future of "nonprofit" research corporations tied to the DoD is being severely impeded from both sides. Universities such as Pennsylvania, the University of California, and Princeton have taken a hard look at academic involvement in classified research for the Pentagon. Princeton, with its huge stake in international-relations programming, is even considering cancelling its sponsorship of a key research arm, the Institute for Defense Analysis. On the other side, many of the "hard" engineering types have continued to press their doubts as to the usefulness of software research. And this barrage of criticism finds welcome support among high military officers who would just as soon cancel social science projects as carry out their implications.

With respect to the panelists, it must be said that a

number of them have indicated their own doubts about the
Report. One of the participants has correctly pointed out
that the Report has not yet been accepted by the DoD, nor
have the findings or the recommendations been endorsed by
the National Academy of Sciences. Another member
claimed that his main reason for accepting the invitation
to serve on the panel was to argue against the Defense
Department's involving universities in operations such as
Project Camelot. He went on to point out that his mission
was unsuccessful, since he obviously did not influence the
other panelists.

A third panelist points out that the Camelot type of
issue was not, to his recollection at least, a criterion in any
discussion of the topics. Yet he strongly disclaims his own
participation as well as membership in the National Academy of Science Advisory Committee on Government Programs in the Behavioral Sciences. He also indicates that
his panel had nothing but an administrative connection
with the National Academy of Sciences, and he, too, seems
to indicate that he had an ancillary advisory role rather
than an integrated preparatory role.

Trying to gauge the accuracy with which the final Report represented a true consensus of the panelists proved
most difficult. While most panelists, with hedging qualifications, agreed that the Report reflected an accurate ap-
praisal of their own views, the question of the actual
writeup of the document brought forth a far from consistent response. One panelist claims that "all members contributed to the basic draft of the Report. Each assumed
responsibility for composing a section, all of which were
then reviewed by the panel as a whole." Another panelist
declared his participation only "as an observer," and that he
was not involved in any final writeup. Yet a third panelist
disclaimed any connection with preparing the Report.

A final, and still different, version was stated as follows: "The report was written by members of the committee and the overall editing and bringing-together responsibility was undertaken by Rains Wallace. One or two members of the committee were assigned to specific topics and drafts were prepared at Williamstown. These went to Wallace, who organized them, did some editing, and sent them back to us. Each person responded and the final version was then prepared by Wallace." In other words, the actual authorship of a document that was released "in confidence" over the names of some of America's most distinguished social scientists is either the work of all and the responsibility of none, or perhaps—as is more likely the case—the work of one or two people and the responsibility of all.

The issuance, even in semiprivate form, of this Report reveals the existence of a wide gap between the thinking of the two chief departments involved in sensitive research and in research in foreign areas—namely, the Department of Defense and the Department of State. Indeed, the issuance of this Report is likely to exacerbate the feelings of high officials in the State Department that the Defense Department position represents an encroachment.

The memorandum issued in December 1967 by the Department of State's Foreign Area Research Coordination group (F.A.R.), in which it set forth foreign-area research guidelines, represents a direct rebuke or, at the very least, a serious challenge to the orientation that the Report of the Defense Science Board represents. It is a high point in federal recognition that real problems do exist.

The F.A.R. Report is broken into two different sections with seven propositions in each section. First, under Guidelines for Research Contract Relations Between Government and Universities, are the following:

(1) The government has the responsibility for avoiding

actions that would call into question the integrity of American academic institutions as centers of independent teaching and research.

(2) Government research support should always be acknowledged by sponsor, university and researcher.

(3) Government-supported contract research should, in process and results, ideally be unclassified, but given the practical needs of the nation in the modern world, some portion may be subject to classification. In this case the balance between making work public or classified should lean whenever possible toward making it public.

(4) Agencies should encourage open publication of contract research results.

(5) Government agencies that contract with university researchers should consider designing their projects so as to advance knowledge as well as to meet the immediate policy or action needs.

(6) Government agencies have the obligation of informing the potential researcher of the needs that the research should help meet, and of any special conditions associated with the research contract, and generally of the agency's expectations concerning the research and the researcher.

(7) The government should continue to seek research of the highest possible quality in its contract program.

A second set of seven recommendations is listed under Guidelines for the Conduct of Foreign Area Research Under Government Contract, and these too bear very directly on the panel Report and do so most critically and tellingly.

(1) The government should take special steps to ensure that the parties with which it contracts have the highest qualifications for carrying out research overseas.

(2) The government should work to avert or minimize adverse foreign reactions to its contract research programs

conducted overseas.

(3) When a project involves research abroad, it is particularly important that both the supporting agency and the researcher openly acknowledge the auspices and financing of research projects.

(4) The government should under certain circumstances ascertain that the research is acceptable to the host government before proceeding on the research.

(5) The government should encourage cooperation with foreign scholars in its contract research program.

(6) Government agencies should continue to coordinate their foreign-area research programs to eliminate duplication and overloading of any one geographical area.

(7) Government agencies should cooperate with academic associations on problems of foreign-area research.

This set of recommendations (with allowances made for the circumstances of their issuance) unquestionably represents the most enlightened position yet taken by a federal agency on the question of the leadership between social science and practical politics. These sets of recommendations not only stand as ethical criteria for the federal government's relationship to social scientists, but—even more decisively—represent a rebuke to precisely the sort of militarization of social science implicit in the panel Report. The reassertion by a major federal policy-making agency of the worth to the government of social science autonomy represented the first significant recognition by a federal agency that Project Camelot was the consequence, not the cause, of the present strains in social science-federal bureaucracy relationships.

May 1968

The Failure of Fail-Safe

JOHN R. RASER

"We have defiled our intellect by the creation of such scientific instruments of destruction that we are now in desperate danger of destroying ourselves. Our plight is critical and, with each effort we have made to relieve it by further scientific advances, we have succeeded only in aggravating our peril. As a result, we are now speeding inexorably toward a day when even the ingenuity of our scientists may be unable to save us from the consequences of a single rash act or a lone reckless hand upon the switch of an uninterceptible missile"

General of the Army Omar N. Bradley, Nov. 5, 1957

Every man—whether poet or pimp, philosopher or philanderer—likes to believe that the work to which he applies his energies is of some value. He may define that value in any number of ways: It uplifts the spirit of man, it serves basic human cravings, it increases man's comprehension of the universe, or it fulfills his own indisputable drives. Most of us, laud-

105

ing consistency more than living it, claim all of the above things at some time, and rationalize our work in terms of any or all of the named values. And like Jeremy Bentham, or like Max Spielman in John Barth's novel *Giles Goat Boy,* we are likely to measure our work by "examining each moment whether what we are doing just now is likely to add to, or detract from, the sum of human misery." It's a tricky and uncertain rule, but it may be the best we can find.

Students of human behavior—behavioral scientists —have special problems in these areas, both because what we study (humankind) is the most precious and volatile element in our world, and because what we discover in our studies can have such a potent effect on the destiny of the very object of study—human beings. Because the study of human behavior is so crucial, and so poorly understood, I should like to outline what behavioral scientists do.

Briefly, we try to understand how human beings act in a variety of situations, by studying them in laboratories and clinics, by using interviews and questionnaires, and by examining historical cases. Some of us go a step further. We interpret what we have learned and apply it to problems of human existence—childrearing, marital relations, racial tensions, poverty, the population explosion, educational policy, or war.

It is this last—war—that is my major interest, and that I wish to discuss. I should like to report on several studies of what happens to human beings in a crisis, then apply the findings of those studies to some aspects of modern warfare. In doing so, I have two objectives. First, I hope to demonstrate that those of us who engage in these difficult and frequently maligned analyses of human behavior sometimes have good reason to believe that our work *is* of value and *does* contribute to the alleviation of human misery; and second, I hope to furnish insights into the crucial role that various assumptions about human behavior can have upon questions of the design of weapons and upon modern military strategy.

I should like to begin by summarizing the findings of several research projects. The first, by James A. Robinson, a professor of political science at Ohio State University, is "Simulating Crisis Decision-Making." The second, "Crises in Foreign Policy Making: A Simulation of International Politics," is by Charles F. Hermann of Princeton University. The third, written at Stanford by Ole R. Holsti, is "Perceptions of Time and Alternatives as Factors in Crisis Decision-Making." The last is a book by physiological psychologist Walter Cannon, *Bodily Changes in Pain, Hunger, Fear and Rage.*

Now, these are jaw-breaking titles and it is obvious from just listing them—without reference to their contents, which are larded with graphs, tables, and formulas—that this is not the type of literature that one keeps on one's coffee table for light reading. Nor are they the kind of document likely to be found in a Congressman's briefcase, a President's chambers, or a general's quarters. But they *are* worth knowing about.

The first two, by Robinson and Hermann, are reports of a complicated laboratory experiment in which military officers acted out the roles of national and military decision-makers in "games" of international affairs. The experimenters introduced crises into the games at various stages—crises that suddenly confronted the officers with intense threats to the achievement of their goals. In studying the officers' behavior in such crises, the experimenters were able to determine that, as a crisis became more intense, the men lost some of their ability to evaluate information, were able to consider fewer alternative courses of action, and tended to be less flexible. In short, as threat increased and time for response decreased, their ability to cope with the situation was lessened.

Holsti's study applied a sophisticated technique of computer analysis to the six-weeks'-long period preceding the outbreak of World War I. His study of the pattern of message flow, and his analysis of the contents of the messages, show plainly that as the crisis intensified, the key governmental and military decision-makers of Austria-Hungary, Germany, England, France, and Russia responded in the same manner as the officers in Robinson and Hermann's laboratory experiment. The decision-makers saw fewer alternatives, they distorted their position in relationship to others, their messages became more stereotyped, and they began to lose the ability to think in long-range terms, focusing their attention instead on extricating themselves from the current problem—and damn the long-range consequences. Thus, as threat intensified, their ability to think and act rationally degenerated, as was true of the officers in the laboratory study.

These studies are among the most recent analyses of the effects of a crisis on decision-making in international relations. Other studies indicate that in most areas of human concern—child-rearing, domestic relations, driving, business, and, indeed, all human activity—conditions of crisis generate similar effects. Panic, terror, hysteria, confusion, anger, and even merely "being rattled" or "upset" can produce these lapses in a person's mental ability. According to the late Harry Stack Sullivan, even the mildest forms of a crisis create

" . . . a considerable degree of imperception, an arrest of constructive, adaptive thinking, and a high degree of suggestibility to almost anything that seems simple and a way out of the difficult situation. There is complete insensitivity to elaborate, difficult suggestions; but the person is relatively impotent to ward off or to resist any simple idea that is given to him."

The point to keep in mind from these three studies, then, is that in times of crisis one is just not able to function as well mentally as one normally does.

The book by Walter Cannon records over 40 years of research on people from several races and cultures. When fear or anger are aroused, he reports, our bodies change. Adrenaline shoots into the bloodstream, the heart speeds up and pumps faster, the muscles expand, the nerves and muscles in the back tense, blood sugar increases, and strength becomes measurably greater. In brief, when faced with a sudden threat, people become—physically—superb fighting machines, far more capable of meeting that threat than otherwise—*if the threat is immediate and physical, and if physical violence is needed to counter it!* Like a cornered rat suddenly transformed into a screeching bundle of fury, launching itself with bared teeth at a man 100 times its size, a desperate and afraid human being turns into a frightening engine of destruction. But as Cannon also points out, while the body gorges itself with strength on account of fear, the mind loses its focus. We think less clearly, we lose our perspective, vision becomes centered on the source of our fear—we are "in a blind rage." Like the rat, we may launch ourselves against an overwhelming adversary, only to go down in "glorious" defeat.

These studies, then, give us a picture supported by much other research. Threat, fear, and rage (crises) *stimulate* us physically but *impair* our mental powers. That's the way we are built, that's how the evolutionary process has coded our glands to operate.

Now I want to change the subject momentarily and discuss the nature of war. Not its value or morality, but its nature. I simply want to describe what it has been like to fight in a war, and how this has changed as we have created sophisticated weaponry to serve our dreams and fears.

Centuries ago, men fought on foot or from horseback, from behind walls and towers. They fought with clubs, knives, spears, swords, bows and arrows, slings, and axes. The Greek or the Hun charged into battle with his every cell inflamed with rage, his heart pounding, adrenaline surging through his veins, his muscles bulging. The defender, too, crouching in his fortress or dashing for his weapon, was suddenly hit with terror, and then rage as he saw the slaughter begin, and he too was transformed into a madly fighting animal. For both, their physiological responses served them well, and their heroic actions became the stuff of epic literature.

More recent developments in weapons mean that the combatants often face one another with guns and flaming jellies. When the man in the trench is suddenly shaken by an exploding shell, or watches his friend's face shattered by a well-placed bullet, rage hits him, his body responds, and his thinking blanks. Screaming vengeance, he may charge suicidally into a hail of machine-gun fire, or dash to toss a grenade into a gunnery nest, or singlehandedly disarm a tank with stones or Molotov cocktails. Again, occasional success is the result. More often, on account of such new death-dealing devices, the outcome is horrible death. Man's instinctual reactions are beginning to conflict with his own cleverness in creating weapons—and are serving him less well. But usually only a few die, so, such incidents, while sad, are probably not important in the scheme of the universe.

But with some types of modern weapons, infinitely greater power has been placed in the hands of the individual. The strategic-bomber pilot over Germany or North Vietnam with his load of TNT or napalm, winging towards his industrial or military target, consults a hundred instruments, a dozen charts, groggily remembers a morning briefing, co-ordinates his crew. Now the defenders react—fighters dive from above, flak and missiles ascend from below. Fear clutches the pilot's heart, rage clouds his vision, he is less able to think clearly, he forgets his information, he tries desperately to get out of trouble—his pounding heart, pulsing veins, and tense muscles are not an aid to him at all, but a hindrance, while his impaired mental power makes him a less, not more, effective fighting man. The result may be, and often is, a blanket of death dumped in fury or error on an innocent hamlet, an empty field, or on the pilot's own troops. No longer is the man whose reasoning power collapses in a crisis the only one to suffer; now others must pay the price. And if the man whose judgment falters under pressure is not a bomber pilot but a chief of state, as in 1914, the world might be plunged into war and several million people might die. But again, in a limited war using conventional weapons, the destruction is nowhere near total. Fifty years after the armistice, the war has lost its sharp outlines, new problems have plagued the world, and the race of man goes on.

When untold nuclear firepower is added to the equation, however, the outcome is different. In our preoccupation with jungle and paddy war in Vietnam, we have let this fact recede to the backs of our minds, but there is another—and all-encompassing—spectre of violence dominating our world. That spectre consists of arsenals of nuclear destruction designed to deter the very holocaust they render possible. To the brains and judgments of individual men has been coupled the power of the suns. Belligerents confront one another across the world—hostile, angry, fearful, threatening and being threatened—and the world is always on the brink of crisis. No longer does the nuclear warrior face his enemy man to man; now he is tangled in a vast complex of gadgets. He is expected to be a servomechanism to electronic devices, a brain plugged into a vast machine, a single circuit in an endlessly complex chain of command. He has been physically emasculated and intellectually extended. His is the brain, the decision unit; but the mechanical extensions of his senses and of his muscles embrace the globe.

Having now reported some behavioral-science research findings on human reactions to threat and crisis, and having sketched the changing nature of man's role in warfare, I should like to combine the two discussions. In doing so, I hope to show how these human reactions may confound the intent and functioning of these weapons systems. I will use just one example—

that of the nuclear submarine, usually considered the most reliable deterrence instrument in the American arsenal.

Forty-one of these Polaris submarines prowl the depths of the oceans, each carrying more explosive power than has been expended in the history of warfare. Each is linked to headquarters by radio waves. Each is commanded by officers chosen for their reliability. In 1964 some strategists began to question that reliability, suggesting that it might be safer if there were some kind of electronic lock-up of the missiles, a lock-up that could be released only by radio signal from headquarters—a Permissive Action Link, as it was designated. The Navy's response was an outraged assertion that these officers had been carefully selected, painstakingly trained, and continually tested, and that they could be totally trusted to behave responsibly— *never* to fire unless ordered to and *always* to fire if ordered to. And the admirals won the dispute. The PAL proposal was dropped and, following a large-scale rescreening program of the Strategic Air Command and Navy personnel who occupied key positions, the assumption was "bought" that the men were a totally reliable component in the decision system.

As we have seen, this very assumption may have been wrong. It may be wrong even with the safeguard of the most sophisticated selection and testing programs. Bruno Bettelheim, a psychiatrist who spent two years in Dachau and Buchenwald, reports of his fellow-prisoners that:

"The way a person acted in a showdown could not be deduced from his inner, hidden motives, which, likely as not, were conflicting. Neither his heroic nor his cowardly dreams, his free associations or con-

114 / JOHN R. RASER

scious fantasies permitted correct predictions as to whether, in the next moment, he would risk his life to protect the life of others, or out of panic betray many in a vain effort to gain some advantage for himself."

The same is true of military officers. Roy Grinker and John Spiegel, psychiatrists who conducted studies of aircraft combat crews during World War II, reported the results of interviews, as well as the results of their intensive testing program. They concluded:

". . . no matter how 'normal' or 'strong' an individual is, he may develop a neurosis if crucial stress impinging on him is sufficiently severe. . . . Furthermore, it has been learned that the important psychological predispositions to 'operational fatigue' are usually latent and therefore difficult to detect until they are uncovered by catastrophic events. It must be concluded that for the vast majority the *only test for endurance of combat is combat itself.*"

They go on to state that military-security regulations prohibit their giving statistics as to how often soldiers collapse during combat!

Surely, you might say, the skills of selection boards and psychiatric procedures have been improved in the more than 20 years since the end of World War II. But not according to two of the men responsible for the Navy's selection and testing program. Captain R.L. Christy and Commander J.E. Rasmussen write that:

". . . the information which is available suggests that the present-day program is not nearly as effective as it was during World War II. . . . Moreover, the general training and experience level of psychiatrists and clinical psychologists assigned to these activities has generally decreased since the end of the Korean War."

They point out that "the program is least effective with high-level personnel where the examiner is faced with complex personality structures and sophisticated defense mechanisms," and conclude that:

"In simplest terms, it is unrealistic to expect any examiner to identify a reasonably well integrated individual's Achilles' heel and the unique combination of emotional and situational factors which could render him ineffective in the unforeseeable future."

What are the implications of this for nuclear weapons systems and their control personnel? The authors state that:

"When the manpower supply is plentiful, it well may be wise to adopt rather high and rigid psychiatric assessment standards for use with men assigned to nuclear weapons. *Some adjustment of the standards becomes necessary during periods of critical manpower shortage.*" (Emphasis added.)

And finally:

"Isolated instances exist, such as those recently reported in the press releases on the human-reliability problem, where obviously unfit individuals have been assigned to nuclear-weapons systems and subsequently have been responsible for potentially disastrous situations. There is no question that the majority of these individuals would have been disqualified for such an assignment if they had undergone psychiatric assessment prior to assuming their duties in a nuclear-weapons system. However, it has been the authors' experience that *the most potentially dangerous situations in the Navy have involved personnel who demonstrated no evidence of psychiatric disturbance at the time of their initial assignment to militarily sensitive duties.* Moreover, as a rule these individuals function in a highly effective fashion for a considerable length of time prior to developing psychiatric illness. Quite frequently, in retrospect, one could not have anticipated that the illness would have developed in this particular group of patients even though the presence of certain underlying psychopathology might have been recognized."

This, then, is the reality behind the military public-relations programs that would persuade us that we can "sleep tight tonight" since our fates are in the hands of infallibly reliable guardians. But behind the public facade, the military has also apparently recognized the frailty of man, for most weapons systems have been hedged with some sort of "fail-safe" arrangement. With the Polaris, for example, only after receiving a sequence of radio signals may a submarine commander fire his missiles at predetermined targets. And this firing requires that several men perform coordinated tasks. The captain and his crew are *never* supposed to decide on their own to fire those missiles. They *can*— it's technically possible—but they aren't supposed to. The captain must *coordinate* the efforts of a group of subordinates in order to fire the missiles, the assumption being that if the captain loses his judgmental ability, the others will retain theirs and thus prevent a mistaken firing.

Yet this assumption, too, is probably wrong. These are men who are chosen for compatibility, who have worked and thought and reasoned together. Chances are very good that they will react in the same way to any crisis. Grinker and Spiegel discuss the intense emotional bonds that grow among combat crews and the almost mystical sense of trust and interdependence that develops, concluding that "From a psychological point of view, the combat leader is a father and the men are his children." And even if the subordinates have doubts, there is research showing that they will most probably obey their captain's order. Paul Torrance has conducted research on B-26 crews and finds that when there is disagreement among them on a correct solution to a problem, the captain nearly always carries the others with him, regardless of whether his decision is "objectively" right or wrong. German officers obeyed, almost to the last man, even though many of them could not have truly accepted Hitler's doctrines. Laboratory subjects will obey an experimenter's instructions to the point of inflicting (so they think) intense electrical shocks on another subject, simply because an experimenter instructs them to do so "for the purposes of the research." When asked later why they did it, the subjects responded, with surprise at the question, "Why, we were told to." The drive to obey an authority seen as legitimate is almost overwhelming—even among students! How much stronger it must be for a military man not to behave mutinously when the "authority" is his senior officer.

My main point, however, is that these men control immense destructive power—and that they alone can check its use. Nothing but the sanity and cool judgment of *all* such key men in the world keep us alive today. Not only submarine commanders, but heads of state, secretaries of defense, radar observers, generals, and bomber-wing and missile-complex commanders must be able to think rationally, interpret information correctly, and act responsibly—keep cool heads in crisis after crisis, and wait patiently and soberly during times of calm. And it must be *all* of them.

This is the way the world is—poised on the brink of destruction because of the assumption that we can rely on the wisdom and cool judgment of these men at all times. Let me sketch a playlet demonstrating the possible consequences of our having failed to make an examination of that assumption before we acted on it.

Both the Soviet Union and the United States (not to mention France, Great Britain, China, and a dozen other countries that may soon join them) have long-range bombers, intercontinental missiles, shorter-range bombers and missiles, and fleets of submarines, all carrying arsenals of nuclear weapons and all under the control of men who must use their good judgment about striking or holding. Let's place our cast of actors on the submarines, since we started with them and since they are often touted as the most error-proof weapons system. If it's *conceivable* that an accident could occur with Polaris, leading to a decision that leads to an unintended war, then the danger is even greater with B-52s, Minuteman missile complexes, and short-range strike forces operating in the European corridors.

The United States and the Soviet Union also have been trying very hard to find ways of detecting these submarines so they cannot remain invulnerable in war. Suppose that in about 1970—in the midst of a Pueblo-like crisis—the Soviet Union responds by asserting that its own intelligence efforts are not inferior to those of the United States, that it has just perfected a radical new means of detecting submerged Polaris submarines. The United States, unwilling to believe this and afraid of domestic and allied reaction, denies that the Soviet Union has succeeded. The Soviet leaders, facing internal critics of the country's unaggressive stance over Vietnam, decide to demonstrate their military potency to the United States, the power of their technology to the world, and their vigorous leadership to their own people. They daringly plan to knock out one Polaris in such a way that everyone will be pretty certain that they did it, but no one could prove it. (Recall the Thresher incident if you like.) They track a submarine with one of their location ships (a fishing trawler); they find its range in the depths of the Indian ocean; they launch a salvo of long-range torpedoes. What they don't know is that the United States has made some recent sonic advances of its own. The submarine detects the oncoming torpedoes and takes evasive action, so it is not the "clean kill" upon which the attacker had relied, but a "near miss." The torpedoes explode, the submarine's hull is damaged, water begins to flood in, panic hits the crew. All is chaos. The men know they will die in a few minutes. The officers, on the basis of instrument readings, are certain that the Polaris has been hit by the Russians, but due to the damage, the depth at which they are cruising, and the attacker's jamming, they cannot establish radio contact with headquarters. Visions of mushroom clouds turning their families into ashes, visions that have haunted their minds for months, suddenly well to the surface; rage explodes in their bodies. Their hearts begin to pound, adrenaline shoots into their blood streams, their muscles expand, their breathing rates accelerate, their blood-sugar levels increase, their muscular strength nearly doubles—but . . . to what end? There is no charging foe, no soul-curdling yell to let out; there are only rows of cold buttons to push. Their reasoning falters, they can't think of alternatives, their memories function inadequately, they can't accurately process information coming in over their meters, they lose track of the long-term perspective and begin to act reflexively. The captain gives the command—"We must accomplish our mission. We will not die in vain." The crew, stunned and equally irrational, obeys.

The final act thus begins. The submarine is desperately trimmed for firing. The missiles lift from their capsules. Suddenly every decision level is in crisis, from radar observer to premier, and reflexes replace reflection. The Soviet Union, now under real attack, despairingly begins to retaliate; the United States orders its counterforce strike; the macabre dance of death unfolds, and in a few hours the world has been reduced to radioactive rubble. There are survivors, but the final curtain of dust does its work well; in a few generations the genetic key has been cruelly twisted, the race of man retreats into mutant extinction, the insects begin their rule of the next geological epoch.

This particular scenario is dramatic and unlikely. It is also tragic and possible. Five nations have thousands of separate weapons systems spread over the world, each with individual command units. As early as 1960, an authoritative report indicated that U.S. nuclear systems had already suffered 10 major accidents and about 50 minor ones—and this, of course, did not include the Thresher incident, the U-2 crashes, Vietnam activities, or nuclear bombs dropped off Spain and Greenland. Premier Khrushchev reportedly told Richard Nixon about an erratic Soviet missile that was destroyed by a signal from the ground as it headed toward Alaska, and on another occasion he implied that military commanders, on their own initiative, could order an attack on American U-2 bases. And these realities obtain in only a short period of time, and with the most "responsible" and sophisticated nuclear powers! In a few years there will be many more such nations. How much compounded will the chance of such crises be when Indonesia, Egypt, Israel, or South Africa have their own primitive nuclear complexes to reinforce their local quarrels? And we may be sure that the experience and technology of every other country will not match the expertise that provides the safeguards incorporated into a Polaris.

Coupling the individual human being to the power of the suns has meant that man's physiological response to crisis may no longer be functional—it may be a tragic flaw. He has become an unwitting victim of his own clever machinations. Now that we have attached our brains to intricate machines of near limitless power, and swaddled our tumescent bodies in frustrating physical inaction, even in the thick of warfare, man may become a self-destroying misfit.

This conceivable scenario with even the relatively foolproof Polaris highlights two basic assumptions on whose accuracy the fate of the world may rest: (1) that carefully selected men will retain cool judgment in an intense crisis, and (2) that even if one man fails, others will act as a "fail-safe" device. Yet, as I have demonstrated, *behavioral-science research shows that both assumptions are almost certainly false.*

We have been trapped, trapped by our egos, into believing that under any conditions we human beings can control both ourselves and the limitless machines to which we attach ourselves. This belief grew out of 17th-century rationalism, and has been reinforced by our spectacular success in mastering our environment.

And we *are* good—damned good—at creating a world in our image and in controlling that world. But there are little foxes, fragile seams, weak links, Achilles' heels, endemic to the human condition, and it well behooves us to lower our ego defenses enough to hear the voices of those who have examined human behavior at its extremes—the kind of extremes that can face decision-makers upon whose infallibility we rely. Sometimes these voices can tell us not only where we are making mistakes, but how we might rectify them.

In 1965 I suggested that the Polaris submarines retain their 1200-mile range missiles rather than getting 2500-mile range missiles; and that they be kept "off-station" or out of range of their targets by several hours' sailing time. This would mean that they *could* be used as retaliatory threats (which is what we claim they are for), but that they would *not* be in the provocative position of being able to strike first without warning, and that they could *not* cause a terrible escalation of the kind of incident I have just described. The responses from military and governmental personnel were that this was an intriguing idea, but since it would mean that Polaris could not be used in a "counterforce" role, the idea could not be taken seriously (as if the use of Polaris in counterforce targeting were somehow decreed by God, or as if counterforce strategies themselves had been proven desirable); or that it was "too late," since the long-range missiles were already in production; or that it would be pointless unless all of our weapons systems could receive the same treatment. In short, the reaction was one of unwillingness to cope with the really difficult problems, a response of fatalistic resignation to the uncontrollability of our destinies, and of detachment from the horror that we may be hastening.

National decision-makers must decide how to build weapons systems; they must decide whether to rely on "nuclear deterrence" or some other strategy. They must make endless assumptions (often unconsciously) about what people are like, how people will respond to crisis, to threat, to rage, to boredom, to too much or too little information, and so on and on. But it is not their business to read endless and often badly written research reports; it is beyond their scope to understand the complex scientific methods used in exposing the intricate dynamics of human behavior. Thus, these decision-makers often act in ignorance—they make false assumptions.

The scholar—the serious student of human behavior, like Robinson, Hermann, Holsti, Cannon, and myself—believes that someone must be responsible for examining policy in the light of the things we are learning about how human beings function. We believe we are failing in our mission unless we tap the policy-maker on the shoulder and tell him we have reason to believe that he is making an unjustified assumption or an erroneous decision. And if he fails to respond to the tap, some of us believe we need to use whatever skills we can generate to collar and shake him, to shout in his ear—to *make* him listen. Otherwise, we are being irresponsible in our role as scholars.

What I have said in the last few pages is just one "minor" illustration of the kind of contribution we can make. Polaris *has* been improved over the years, on the basis of the designers' better understanding about the complexities of human behavior. It is far more difficult to devise a credible "accidental war" scenario now than it was in 1960—or 1965.

But many issues—from other, less stable weapons systems to negotiating strategies, from our policy towards China, or in Vietnam, to race relations or population growth—are crying for analysis and understanding. We behavioral scientists are not simply teaching industry how to administer personality tests better, or teaching the Defense Department how to design a bomber cockpit better, or teaching the Peace Corps how to train a volunteer better.

In many instances we are digging up information that is revolutionary—information that may suggest that a radical revision is necessary in the basic policy assumptions of our nation's decision-makers, and of decision-makers throughout the world.

January 1969

FURTHER READING SUGGESTED BY THE AUTHOR:

Arms Control for the Late Sixties by James E. Dougherty and J. F. Lehman, Jr. (Princeton, N.J.: Princeton University Press, 1967) is a study of current problems of arms control.

Sanity and Survival: Psychological Aspects of War and Peace by Jerome D. Frank (New York: Random House, 1968) applies psychological and other behavioral science findings to issues of deterrence and the control of nuclear weapons.

Nuclear Weapons, Missiles, and Nuclear War: Problems for the Sixties by Charles A. McClelland (San Francisco: Howard Chandler, 1960) presents a collection of studies on the problems and prospects of the nuclear age.

New Ways to Reduce Distrust Between the United States and Russia

MILTON ROSENBERG

"Nations are not people, and therefore the troubles between them cannot be understood through psychology." So runs a complaint that psychologists often hear from political scientists these days.

This point of view strikes me as both justified and unjustified, depending upon the kind of psychological approach being considered. Worthy of condescension is the sort of shallow psychologizing that suggests that national frustration leads directly to national aggression, or that attempts to explain particular wars as due to the madness of some specific historical figure or the basic personality structure of a whole people.

Another approach to the psychology of international relations, however, has been quietly maturing over the last decade. This approach assumes that the interests of various nations are frequently in real conflict—but that it is also common for international rivalries of the war-risking kind to be based largely upon attitudes that have no clear factual support. A guiding purpose in this new approach is to achieve a better understanding of the psychological forces that tend to drive both types of conflict toward limited, and then unlimited, war.

One important development is the attempt to focus some of the major theories of attitude change upon the relations between national élites. This may point ways out of dangerous international antagonisms that are rooted mainly in attitudes. And even where the clash of national interests is apparently "intractable," the alteration of background attitudes may still point ways out of the dilemma.

In this article, I hope to show how two of the major theories of attitude change might be applied in lowering some of the barriers to realistic settlement of international issues.

For simplicity I shall deal mainly with the interaction between the American and Soviet policy élites. But what is suggested here could be readily applied to aspects of the U.S.-Chinese or the Soviet-Chinese relationships—or, for that matter, to those of Israel and Egypt or any other set of national élites locked into mutual disdain and suspicion but not yet caught in long-term regression to active war, as we now are in Vietnam.

The *instrumental-learning* model of attitude dynamics was developed by Carl I. Hovland and Irving L. Janis and their associates, first in field experiments conducted for the Army during World War II and then at Yale. At its core is the idea that we learn to like or dislike (or to trust or distrust) someone or something by *reinforcement*—that is, because in the past the expression of our like or dislike has brought us rewards or reduced our needs.

The largest amount of experimental study has been devoted to two types of rewards. One is tied directly to what a person can gain if he changes some specific attitude—for instance, a person could reduce his anxiety over his health if he adopted an uncompromisingly negative attitude toward smoking. The second type of reward is due to increased social acceptance gained by moving one's attitudes toward the attitudinal standards set by others. Usually this happens not through mere cynical compliance, but through a gradual and "internalized" reorientation.

Changing the attitude of another person, according to this model, requires a series of steps:
—attract the attention of the person or groups whose attitudes you want to change;
—establish your credibility and trustworthiness;
—provide well-planned and informative communications that cast doubt upon the reasons and rewards that bolster the present attitude, and make change seem desirable by highlighting the rewards associated with the new, advocated attitude; and
—get the person or group to "rehearse" the new attitude for a while—to make its promised rewards seem more real and immediate.

Experimental work conducted by the Yale group and others has identified a number of factors that determine the success with which the various stages are negotiated. Among them are the basic credibility of the source of the persuasive communication; the way in which the communication is structured; the use of anxiety arousal; "role-playing" as a way of getting the person to consider the arguments and incentives that support the new attitude; the importance to the person of groups that support his attitude or its opposite; and personality factors making for general persuadability or rigidity.

Clearly, this model is relevant to changing the attitude pattern of distrust that continues to hamper movement toward true American-Soviet conciliation. The policy élites involved are composed of men playing roles that reduce flexibility. What limits these men most is that they feel *required* to distrust the opposing power and the assurances offered by its élite. Yet each side recognizes that the other's attitude of distrust must be converted toward trust if anything better than an easily-upset détente is to be achieved. Specifically, each side faces the problem of getting the other to believe its assurances that it will refrain from a surprise nuclear attack; that it will abide by arms-control and disarmament agreements (even when these cannot be effectively policed); that it will scrupulously adhere to sphere-of-influence agreements; and that it will accept necessary limitations of sovereignty as new and powerful international institutions are developed.

How are such attitudes of trust to be cultivated while policy élites still pursue and protect national interests? How can the Soviet-American "credibility gap" be closed?

The Yale experiments on credibility indicated that what seems to count most are the communicator's apparent status and expertise. But these have little bearing upon relations between policy-élite representatives, who are usually perceived by their opposite numbers as possessing both of these qualities in more than sufficient degree.

At this level there is, however, a more direct route

toward cultivating attitudes of trust. Though difficult to pursue, it must be taken, even while each nation strives to preserve and advance its own national interests. That route, to speak bluntly, is to stop posturing, faking, and lying.

Is it possible—even conceivable—that nations, in their relations with one another, can abandon the deceit that, since Machiavelli, has seemed essential to statecraft? Many specialists would immediately answer, in the tones of revealed doctrine, "As it was in the beginning, is now, and ever shall be, world without end. Amen." But at the risk of sounding naive, I believe that we need take a fresh look.

I suggest that the present international system is so inadequate and dangerous that the American and Soviet leaders have very compelling reasons to go beyond the limits of conventional *Realpolitik* and impose some moral order on their relationships. The exploration of this radical possibility could best begin with a direct assault upon the attitudinal problem of international distrust. There are probably many ways in which the behavioral sciences might help to mount such an assault. One would be the use of inter-nation gaming and simulation techniques—to provide "dry run" tests of an international system based upon a principle of generalized trust. Such studies might clarify just how feasible, how resistant to breakdown, a system of this sort would be, and how it might best be instituted.

But we need not wait. Immediate initiatives in honesty and self-revelation are now available for the seizing. Even though a great deal remains secret, even though the international system remains more closed than open, much could still be revealed to an antagonist under conditions that would allow him the opportunity for verification. There are possibilities in the direct revelation of data about arms technology, economic plans, the policy-formulation process itself. Such candor might well invite reciprocation. It might, in fact, set in motion expanding cycles of reciprocity that could eventually encompass most of the matters now surrounded by suspicion.

Another way of attempting to reduce attitudes of distrust would be, simply, to seek occasions that will require promises to be given—particularly promises that seem to incur some disadvantage for the promiser —and then to make sure that they are conscientiously fulfilled. This serves as almost incontrovertible evidence of reliability and credibility.

Additional useful suggestions can be drawn from the work of the Hovland group when we consider their emphasis (well backed by many experimental studies) upon appeals to the motives and incentives of individuals. How does this translate to the situation of one élite communicating with another? It highlights the importance of conducting diplomatic interaction so as to make clear to the other side the gains that are available if it will undertake an accommodating shift on some issue under negotiation.

This recommendation applies not so much to the general goal of reducing attitudes of distrust as to the conciliation of more specific issues. What if the United States offered the Soviet Union something it wanted in return for an arms quarantine of the Middle East? Or what if the Soviet Union offered us some equally meaningful reward for a U.S. guarantee that West Germany would not be allowed access to nuclear arms? In either instance the consequence might be conciliatory yielding. This would be due to changes of attitudes on the particular issues. But an exchange of such yieldings, particularly if accompanied by the recurring experience of promises kept, could alter the more basic attitudes of distrust that still persist between the American and Soviet policy-making groups.

Why, then, has this approach to conciliation rarely been used? One reason: Ingrained attitudes of mutual distrust inhibit easy exploration and flexible exchanges of conciliatory shifts. Another: The incentives occasionally offered to change attitudes are usually negative, not positive—threats and harassment, not attractive rewards. Leaders on either side may sometimes be forced to bow to such pressures, but their distrust and hostility will hardly diminish. Just the opposite: The élite group forced to yield, especially if humiliated, will await its opportunities for retribution.

The United States and Russia will continue to try to control each other's attitudes and actions by negative means as long as their leaders view their relationship as an extended zero-sum game—one side can win only if the other loses. Some issues, of course, are zero-sum; but many can be so structured that mutual gain *is* possible. Peace itself, after all, is a mutual gain.

Still, it is clear that possibilities for mutual gain cannot be found in each and every conflict. It would be better, therefore, to systematically rely on cross-trading. In other words, the advantage in one interest conflict is given to one side, while the advantage in another conflict is given to the other side. For example, the Soviet Union's refusal to allow unlimited inspection of its atomic facilities, and the United States' commitment to some form of nuclear force within NATO, are both seemingly unbudgeable stances. Might full, unscheduled inspections in the Soviet Union be traded for the permanent cancellation of plans for a NATO nuclear force?

The opportunities are vast. Both sides could continually review their priorities. How strongly do they desire particular concessions? What are they willing to offer in trade? Permanent trade-off negotiations could lead to large and thoroughgoing patterns of settlement.

After some initial success in trade-off negotiations, both groups would have experienced gains: The reduction of tensions, and domestic improvements made possible by shifting economic resources away from the defense sector. These gains would probably foster additional significant change in the attitudes of competitiveness and distrust that presently impede progress in American-Soviet conciliation. And this, in turn, would be likely to produce, on both sides, the strengthened conviction that trade-off negotiations are generally profitable even though they require abandonment of some earlier policy goals.

It would also be very useful if the United States and the Soviet Union were to immediately expand the search for shared problems that do *not* raise the apparent or fundamental issues of the lingering Cold War—problems in such comparatively manageable areas as technological development, scientific techniques, urban design, educational methods, crime control, and administrative organization. An institutionalized system that would foster greater East-West cooperation in the solution of such cross-national, domestic problems would probably be of clear benefit to both nations, as well as to the members of their respective blocs. And this, too, would further invalidate basic attitudes of competitiveness and distrust and foster further progress in resolving issues that have persisted in the framework of Cold War competition.

At least one other recommendation can be drawn from the instrumental-learning model of attitude change. Studies at Yale and elsewhere have shown that role-playing is a direct and effective method of changing attitudes. The subject becomes a kind of devil's advocate: He is required to argue for a viewpoint quite different from his own. In laboratory experiments, this often leads to attitude change—though exactly why and how this happens remains controversial.

In discussions between opposing groups of policy-makers, one would not expect or desire such facile shifts of attitude. But there is good reason to expect that role-playing techniques could help policy-makers of opposed groups to reexamine and, where necessary, revise the attitudes of suspicion and distrust they approach one another with. Further formal research on this process, and real-life experiments with it, would add considerably to the development of a technology of conciliation.

A word of warning is required. When a formerly hostile and untrusting opponent is beginning to change his attitudes, when he is letting his guard down, the temptation to take advantage of his new and tentative trust will often be great. Though short-run strategic and political gains may beckon in such a situation, they must be completely rejected—for nothing will so easily destroy the credibility of conciliatory communications and actions than a lapse into even a single unscheduled seizure of advantage.

The *consistency* theories represent a second major approach to attitude change, and they can add a good deal to our understanding of how to reduce distrust between policy élites. Though they differ in important ways, all these theories see an attitude as a combination of elements bound together in a kind of internal balance, so that any sizable disruption will bring into play a self-regulating dynamic that restores the original harmony. The basic assumptions, then, are that human beings need attitudinal consistency and are intolerant of inconsistency—and that when this consistency is disrupted, they often restore it through the process of attitude change.

So goes the general consistency-theory analysis. But to show its relevance to the problem of inter-élite distrust, we must get down to the particulars of one of the major theories of this type. The one that I will use is my own, though it reflects aspects of a related theory developed in cooperation with Robert Abelson. The fact that I use it here does not mean that it is superior to the other consistency models of attitude change, but simply that it is convenient for probing deeper into the problem of cross-élite attitude change.

Basic to this model is the definition of an attitude as a kind of psychological stance in which elements of *affect* and *cognition* are intimately related. The affective core of the attitude is simply the person's habitual feeling of like or dislike toward some "object," be that a person, an issue, a proposal, an institution, or an event. The cognitive component is simply his total set of beliefs about that liked or disliked object, particularly beliefs about how it is related to other things he is interested in and has feelings about.

To exemplify just what we mean by affective-cognitive consistency, and by the kind of inconsistency that fosters a change of attitude, we need to work through a concrete illustration. Let us take a hypothetical U.S. Senator standing on the periphery of the American decision-making circle just before the ratification of the atmospheric nuclear test-ban treaty. He approves of the treaty and plans to vote for it. This reflects his affective component—how he *feels* about the treaty.

In public debate he gives some of his reasons—the cognitive component: "The ban will slow the nuclear race. It will protect us from radioactive poisoning of the air. It will show the world that we mean it when we say we want peace." Privately, he adds other considerations: "It will probably freeze the nuclear race where it is now, while we still have a big advantage. Also, it should eventually open up some Eastern European markets we can use." Still another of his private reasons: "Judging by the latest polls, my stand should go over well with the liberal church and women's groups back home. Anyway, it should get the White House off my back and maybe get me better support from the National Committee in my next campaign."

If we check all of these reasons (technically, each is a cognition about the relationship between the attitude object and some other emotionally significant object), we find an interesting fact: The attitude object (the test-ban treaty) toward which the Senator has a positive feeling is, to him, positively related to such welcome developments as "opening up some Eastern European markets" and negatively related to such unwelcome possibilities as "radioactive poisoning of the air." This demonstrates a general principle: A positively-evaluated attitude object will typically be seen as bringing about desired goals or preventing undesirable ones; a negatively-evaluated object will be seen as blocking the way to desired goals, or fostering undesirable ones. Such affective-cognitive consistency has often been shown to be characteristic of stable attitudes. Furthermore, research has shown that the stronger and more extreme the basic positive or negative feeling toward the attitude object, the greater will be the person's certainty about the supporting beliefs.

How then, according to this model, can attitudes be changed? One must begin by trying to break up the internal harmony of beliefs and feelings—by inducing, or increasing, inconsistency. Most often, this is attempted by presenting arguments, data, and "facts" from sources that are seen as authoritative because of their prestige or expertise. The purpose is either to undermine beliefs that support the affective core of the attitude ("Experts say we can't be sure of our test-detection system, so how can we know the Russians won't keep testing and get far ahead of us?"), or to introduce new assertions that cast a different light— and thus induce contrasting feelings—on the subject ("If we stop testing, we simply cannot develop a good low yield, antimissile missile").

Introduce enough inconsistency and the subject will no longer be able to tolerate it. How much internal inconsistency a person can stand varies from attitude to attitude, situation to situation, and person to person. But everyone must reach a point where the piling up of inconsistency forces him to try to do something about it.

When a person's internal inconsistency becomes unbearable, one of three things will usually happen:

■ He will simply retreat from the conflict. He will try to find some way to disregard the whole area of inconsistency.

■ He will reject and expel the new cognitions that

are upsetting the old balance, and restore the initial attitude. (Incidentally, we may assume that this is what our hypothetical Senator did, since it is just what many real Senators did. The arguments *against* the nuclear test-ban treaty were simply not so telling and credible, or so important in the values they referred to, as were the arguments in favor of the treaty. In this case, the easiest route to reducing internal inconsistency was, ultimately, to reject the arguments that had generated it.)

■ He will yield to the new inconsistency-arousing cognitions, and—by changing his feelings about the attitude object—restore consistency.

This last is, of course, what is usually meant by attitude change.

Consistency theory also predicts, and has experimentally demonstrated, that the reverse form of attitude change is possible: *Feelings* can be altered first, and cognitions will follow. But, in real life, affect change resulting from prior cognition change is far more common.

What determines whether internal inconsistency brings about an overall change of attitude? First, the nature of the attitude itself. An attitude will probably be more easily changed by inconsistency if:

■ The number of beliefs that support the attitude is small.

■ The attitude object is believed to serve comparatively unimportant goals.

■ The person already holds a few beliefs that are inconsistent with his overall attitude.

■ The original attitude is isolated from most of the other attitudes of the individual—is itself, therefore, in a sense an inconsistency. (An example with a real Senator: Everett M. Dirksen's support of an earlier civil-rights bill was on the periphery of his essentially conservative concerns; his stance on civil rights has since undergone several sea changes.)

A second factor determining whether inconsistency leads to attitude change is how important the attitude is to a person's needs and essential motivations. The less the holding of the attitude serves to meet his real needs, the more easily—if threatened by inconsistency —it can be changed. Similarly, his attitudes are more easily altered when he does not need them for the roles he plays, or for maintaining good standing in the groups he identifies with.

From the foregoing, it is apparent why changing the attitudes of national leaders has been so difficult during the Cold War—even though both sides wanted to find some way out. The core attitudes of distrust, hostility, and competition have been so thoroughly anchored and buttressed by supporting beliefs, so strongly influenced by what leaders think their positions and "roles" require of them, that there has been very little room for flexibility.

This does not mean that evidence of good will or pacific intentions has been totally useless. But what usually happens is that these gestures are reinterpreted in ways that reduce their power to generate inconsistency and thus their power to affect attitudes. For example, an American offer of wheat sales would typically be interpreted by the Russians as a tactic to help the U.S. economy. And American leaders are likely to interpret Soviet offers to share information about industrial nuclear technology as a ploy to save the costs of research—rather than really to further general cooperation. Many leaders traditionally interpret gestures for peace as a mask for hostile intent—and bellicose gestures as proof of it.

Perhaps, therefore, the greatest positive good that came from the few very dangerous confrontations between the United States and the Soviet Union—particularly the Cuban missile crisis—has been that they gave the leaders of both nations some appreciation of how deeply each wanted to avoid stumbling into nuclear war. Since then, a number of steps toward avoiding danger have been taken, and they have probably thrown some inconsistency into the attitudes of mutual distrust. As a result, there is probably a fair opportunity today for each side to act in ways that could ultimately bring about changed attitudes. How can this best be done? The consistency approach offers some leads.

One clear recommendation is that, before the competing policy groups undertake to revise each other's attitudes, they study what these attitudes really are, and what beliefs are built into them. Too often policymakers seem confused about the perceptions and purposes that lie behind the policy positions taken by the competing power. "Riddles wrapped in mysteries inside enigmas" lie more often in the eye of the observer than the observed. Surely, within the great mass of white papers, diplomatic conversations, propaganda releases, and policy rationalizations that flow from Washington or Moscow there should be enough material for an educated reconstruction of how opposing leaders really think and feel about an issue, and how they structure policy around it. Close study of this sort would help isolate the issues on which the other side would be comparatively receptive to actions and messages that could generate internal inconsistency.

Obviously these issues, at the present time, would

be on the outer edge of major policy and have little immediate effect on important conflicts. But the real purpose of such early efforts is to lower the opposing side's defense against information and action that might create inconsistency in more central attitudes. If either side could convince the other that it really *does* favor cultural exchange in order to reduce tension, rather than to make propaganda—or that it really *wants* disengagement in Central Europe to avoid military confrontations, rather than to gain some devious advantage—then the day will be much closer when the very center of the web of distrust and competition can be directly assaulted.

But can such direct assault succeed when the core issues still seem virtually irreconcilable? How is this to be done? This is where the consistency approach is especially pertinent. It suggests strongly that *there are no truly intractable, unchangeable attitudes.* Instead, there are less resistant and more resistant ones. Where resistance is high, this is because the affective portion of the attitude is supported by a large number of detailed beliefs that are consistent with it—and also because the attitude itself is consistent with the role demands and ideologies that leaders must live up to. For such an attitude to be changed it must be bombarded with a continuing, unrelenting stream of inconsistency-generating communications and events— and the more peripheral attitudes to which it is tied must also be exposed to pressures for change.

To reverse the attitudes of distrust with which the Soviet and American élites approach and misinterpret each other, either or each of them must undertake an unflagging display of trustworthiness—and give strong, unequivocal evidence that its paramount desire is conciliation. In this light Charles Osgood's GRIT strategy is very relevant. Osgood recommends a long series of unilateral, tension-reducing initiatives on the part of the United States, even if no sign of reciprocation appears from the Soviets for some time. He also maintains that concrete actions speak much louder—and less ambiguously—than words.

For too long both the United States and the Soviet Union have been lagging in this regard. On the American side, occasional actions in the Kennedy years and in the last period of the Eisenhower era may have worked, whether by intention or not, to generate some inconsistencies in Soviet core attitudes of distrust. But these actions were never designed as part of a strong, well-focused plan for reducing tension. Today the situation is worse. What probably stands out most to the Soviets is our past escalation of the Veitnam war and our continuing rejection of those opportunities for realistic settlement that are apparently available.

Still other recommendations can be drawn from the consistency approach, particularly from the variants developed by other authors. Here is one example out of a number of possibilities: Both Fritz Heider and Theodore Newcomb have studied the kind of consistency that is found *between* rather than *within* the attitudes of separate people. And both have reported considerable supporting evidence for this proposition: People who are tied together by friendship or more formal role relationships tend toward mutual consistency on important attitude issues. Nevertheless, they will sometimes encounter inconsistency between their separate attitudes. When this happens, the formally or emotionally subordinate person will usually alter his attitude to bring it into consistency with that of the other person.

This proposition is not surprising, but put this way it does have considerable practical value. What it suggests is that attempts to produce attitude change through arousing inconsistency will work best if we first learn as much as possible about members of the "target group" and their relationships with one another. Who are the key men, why, and what are they like?

The most influential, in governmental as in business élites, are not always the most visible. When we know who the crucially placed people in the opposing élite are—and, particularly, when their importance is based upon their analytic or strategic skills—we have found the people toward whom our initial attempts at inconsistency arousal ought to be especially directed. If *their* attitudes begin to shift, the effect may spread across the élite group more rapidly than could otherwise happen.

In all that I have said up to now I have been urging greater adventurousness in the attempt to reduce inter-élite distrust. But, of course, real-life constraints and responsibilities often inhibit the taste for adventure and innovation. The policy-élite groups of the contesting powers are still limited by their attitudes of distrust toward one another, and by concerns over the domestic political consequences of a too rapid or dramatic movement toward international conciliation. Also they are sometimes hampered by the "prudential" (the word is borrowed from certain strategic analysts) definition of their roles—that is, they sometimes take it as their obligation to imagine the worst they can about the opposing power's motives and intentions and then to act on the assumption that what they have imagined is accurate.

Thus most of the suggestions made here would probably not be acceptable to typical members of the policy élites of the contesting powers. However, desperation over the impasse imposed by the Cold War, and fear of escalation, have moved some leaders to re-examine their own attitudes about the plans and intentions of their opposite numbers. This development had, in fact, progressed quite far—until it began to languish and lose relevance in the wake of the Vietnam war.

If the Vietnam war should end with a setback for those American policy-makers still committed to the John Foster Dulles "roll-back of Communism" and "brinksmanship" doctrines, we may see an energetic renewal of the search for meaningful conciliation. Awareness of the possibilities discussed here could make that search much more productive. And in the meantime it can foster preparation for new peace initiatives and help to keep alive the prospect of ultimate conciliation.

April 1968

FURTHER READING SUGGESTED BY THE AUTHOR:

Communication and Persuasion by Carl I. Hovland and Irving L. Janis (New Haven, Conn.: Yale University Press, 1953).

An Alternative to War or Surrender by Charles Osgood (Urbana, Ill.: University of Illinois Press, 1963).

Attitude Organization and Change by Milton J. Rosenberg, Carl I. Hovland, *et al.* (New Haven, Conn.: Yale University Press, 1960).

International Behavior: A Social-Psychological Analysis edited by Herbert C. Kelman (New York: Holt, Rinehart & Winston, 1965). See "Images in Relation to the Policy Process—American Public Opinion on Cold-War Issues" by Milton J. Rosenberg.

ABM and the Arms Race

MARVIN KALKSTEIN

In recent months there has been extensive discussion and debate of the ABM issue, and it has been generally recognized as one of the key issues presently facing the nation. On Friday, March 14, 1969, President Nixon announced the administration's decision with regard to ABM. Now it remains for Congress and the public to determine where we go from here.

With the Presidents' announcement, we now have a set of specific recommendations and arguments upon which to focus our attention. The President suggested that the proposed deployment is designed to fulfill three objectives:

1) protection of our land-based retaliatory forces against direct attack by the Soviet Union

2) defense of the American people against the kind of nuclear attack that Communist China is likely to be able to mount within the decade

3) protection against the possibility of accidental attack from any source

Let us first look at the question of protecting our land-based retaliatory forces. The President has said that "the imperative that our nuclear deterrent remains secure beyond any possible doubt requires that the United States must take steps now to insure that our strategic retaliatory forces will not become vulnerable to Soviet attack." It should be recognized that our present deterrent is comprised of a mix of nuclear-weapons systems including, according to Defense Department figures as of September 1968, 1,054 land-based intercontinental ballistic missiles, 656 sea-based Polaris missiles on 41 nuclear-powered submarines, and 646 strategic air bombers. This force then consists of 1,710 ballistic missiles and 646 bombers capable of delivering a total of 4,200 nuclear weapons against an enemy. The same source indicates that the Soviet Union possesses 900 land-based ICBMs, 45 sea-based ballistic missiles, and 150 strategic air bombers capable of carrying a total of about 1,200 nuclear warheads. According to Defense Department estimates, even as few as 200 delivered warheads could cause 50 million Soviet fatalities and destroy 70 percent of their industry. Thus, it should be obvious that present Soviet forces do not pose a credible threat to our retaliatory forces. Concern for the security of our retaliatory forces seems to stem from the fact that the Soviet Union reached its present level of ICBMs through a large buildup in the past two or three years.

The main argument supporting this contention that the Soviet Union is striving to achieve a first-strike capability has been the recent disclosure by Secretary of Defense Melvin Laird of intelligence information regarding the Soviet deployment of the SS-9 missile, thought to be capable of carrying nuclear warheads with a yield as large as

20 or 25 megatons. Other estimates put the size of the warhead at five-ten megatons. Since the main advantage in using high-yield warheads would be to attack hardened missile sites rather than cities, Laird has cited their deployment as evidence of Soviet first-strike intentions. However, the number of SS-9 missiles currently deployed is given as 200 and on the basis of the recent rate of deployment, it is predicted that the number will reach 500 in 1975.

Neither of these numbers represents a credible first-strike potential; indeed, what is truly incredible is the suggestion that the United States deterrent force is suddenly to become wholly inadequate. Even equipping the SS-9 with Multiple Independently Targetable Re-entry Vehicles (MIRVs) will not change this picture, as I will discuss later. Furthermore, former Secretary of Defense Clark Clifford was aware of the same intelligence at the time of his January 15, 1969, defense-posture statement, and he was neither unduly alarmed nor as prone to predict so many Soviet SS-9 weapons in 1975. He felt that their deployment would probably soon level off. The recent build-up, he stated, was most likely motivated more from a desire to achieve parity with United States forces rather than an attempt to arrive at a first-strike capability against our forces.

Apart from the SS-9, there appears to be further concern in the Administration based upon the Soviet's having achieved a capability of producing a sizeable number of submarines equipped with ballistic missiles. At the indicated rate of seven submarines a year, however, it will be many years before this force equals ours. They may be regarded as a threat to our land-based bombers, since they might afford a shorter warning time. But the Perimeter Acquisition Radar (PAR) would be to some extent helpful as a means of affording early warning.

Another factor cited by the President in the buildup of Soviet strategic forces is their development of the Fractional Orbital Bombardment System (FOBS). FOBS are recognized as having very low accuracy and therefore cannot properly be regarded as a threat to our hardened land-based missiles. They may, however, represent a threat to our bomber forces. By using a low orbit, it is possible that they could reduce the warning time that we would have from our Ballistic Missile Early Warning System (BMEWS), thus making it more difficult to get our aircraft airborne before their bases are struck. However, according to former Secretary Clifford, it would not reduce the possibility of early detection by our planned Over-the-Horizon (OTH) and satellite-borne missile warning systems. He suggested as an additional available option that we can increase from 40 to 60 percent the proportion of bombers held on 15-minute ground alert, assuring us of the survival of at least 385 planes capable of delivering more than 10,000 megatons of nuclear explosives.

Probably the most secure component of our retaliatory force is the Polaris submarine fleet. Secretary Laird in his testimony before the Senate Armed Services Committee and the Disarmament Subcommittee of the Foreign Relations Committee on March 20 and 21, 1969, intimated that this security may be threatened by the mid-1970's. However, in no way did he substantiate this possibility. The nation's leading technical experts for years have regarded the Polaris submarine as invulnerable and none as yet have indicated any change in this opinion. The most recent public information is that detection and tracking of these submarines at any substantial distance is still beyond the realm of present technical capability and is likely to remain so for a considerable time into the future. It is obvious.

that unforeseen developments might negate any weapons system we might have, including an ABM system, but such consideration cannot be used as a major basis for defense policy. At least, not if we wish to pursue sound policies.

In discussing our capability against "Greater-Than-Expected Threats," former Secretary Clifford regarded only an extensive, effective Soviet ABM defense as a counter to our submarine-launched missiles. Apparently, he was not as impressed as Secretary Laird with potential Soviet threats to our Polaris submarines. Of our additional available options, one of which allows the expansion of Sentinel to include defense of our Minutemen sites, he stated that, "We need not take any of these steps until we have some evidence that the threat is actually beginning to emerge." Obviously, his assessment of our intelligence information was quite different from Laird's. Or, quite possibly, Secretary Laird's position is based on reasons he has been unwilling to discuss. Clifford concluded that "taking our strategic posture as a whole, we have an ample margin of safety and we can afford to proceed with due deliberation on very costly new programs."

In ruling out increasing the number of sea- and land-based missiles and bombers as a means to insure the survival of our retaliatory forces, the President argued that such a course provides only marginal improvement of our deterrent. This seems indeed to be true but can only be regarded as such by recognizing the fact that our present forces represent an overwhelmingly large deterrent. Quite rightly, with such an overwhelming deterrent, any increase at this time would be of marginal value.

A second option rejected by the President would be to further harden our ballistic missile forces by putting them in more strongly reinforced underground silos. Harold Brown, former Secretary of the Air Force, has described new harder silos as "a form of ABM defense." Increasing the hardness by about a factor of 10 would reduce the probability of one SS-9 destroying a Minuteman missile by from 90 percent to about 20 percent. To regain a 90 percent destruction capability, the Soviet Union would need 10 times as many such weapons as would presently be the case. Converting their SS-9 missiles to MIRVS would not appreciably affect the situation. The probability of destroying a Minuteman with three five-megaton warheads is not much greater than with one 25-megaton warhead. The introduction of superhard silos would, in fact, have a number of advantages for protecting our ICBMs. Since concrete is a main ingredient, it would be much cheaper and far more reliable. I have a high expectation that concrete would do what it is expected to do, whereas the highly complex ABM system could fail for a variety of reasons. Finally, such an approach would not give rise to a new round in the arms race. At the very least, moving to superhard silos should allow us to delay an ABM deployment for a number of years.

Finally, the economics of attempting to provide an effective defense of our land-based missiles should not be overlooked. The present proposed figures for the Safeguard system will allow the deployment of only a relatively small number of Spartan and Sprint missiles at each site. (The Spartan has a 400-mile to 500-mile range and can afford defense coverage to a very large area; the Sprint is a 25-mile to 30-mile range missile that can provide protection against an incoming missile around the terminal point.) The first two ABM sites to be deployed by 1973 are planned to protect our Malmstrom, Montana, and Grand Forks, North Dakota, Minuteman bases, each of which have about 150 Minuteman missiles. On the basis of 700 Spartan missiles in the original Sentinel System, we can expect that 60 to 70 Spartans will be allotted per ABM base. The increased cost for the Safeguard system suggests that a similar number of Sprints may be assigned to each base. The reason for rejecting the Sentinel defense of our cities against Soviet attack is that area defense based only on Spartan will not work against a sophisticated and large attack of the sort that the Soviet Union can launch. Thus the protection of our missiles will depend upon the hardpoint defense provided by the Sprint missiles. Sixty to 70 Sprints can at best provide protection against an equal number of Soviet warheads. Obviously, in 1973 only a handful of our Minuteman missiles will be protected, and it won't be until several years later that the Safeguard system will encompass our full Minuteman force. Even then, its capability to cope with a Soviet first-strike will be questionable.

Should the Soviet Union contemplate a first-strike attack, they would have to use at least as many warheads as we have Minuteman missiles. With less than half as many Sprints as Minutemen, more than half our Minutemen would be virtually unprotected. To protect all our Minutemen (which admittedly may not be a necessary aim), we would need at least as many Sprints. If, as is likely, an attacker would assign more than one warhead per Minuteman to insure himself of a high probability of destroying our Minuteman, we would have to increase the number of Sprints accordingly. Furthermore, if we desire a high probability of destroying an incoming missile, we would have to assign several Sprints for each warhead in their force. Even if our objective is to assure ourselves of the survival of a few hundred Minuteman missiles after an enemy first-strike, the number of Sprints needed may range into the several thousands, requiring the expenditure of tens of billions of dollars for Sprints alone.

Greatly increased expenditures would undoubtedly be

required for the radar and computer components of the system if the system is even to suggest the survival of an adequate retaliatory force. At present, our Missile Site Radars are not sufficiently hardened to withstand the effects of a high-yield airburst. Several incoming warheads targeted on the MSR would stand a good chance of destroying or incapacitating it. Once this has occurred, all the remaining Sprints dependent upon that MSR will have become useless. To avoid this, in addition to greater hardening for the MSRs, considerable expenditures will be required for more MSRs. We would thus be talking about spending tens of billions of dollars just to make it possible that Safeguard has some chance of providing the protection that the President desires.

The President's second proposed objective for his ABM was to protect the American people from a nuclear attack by Communist China. The first line of defense against such an attack is prevention, and that is precisely what our deterrent forces are meant to accomplish. If our deterrent forces can be relied upon to prevent a nuclear attack by a large strategic force of the Soviet Union, they should be more than adequate against the virtually nonexistent strategic nuclear forces of Communist China. In spite of the militant talk by the Chinese and about them, former Secretary of Defense Robert S. McNamara in his September 18, 1967, speech announcing the previous Sentinel decision acknowledged that "China has been cautious to avoid any action that might end in a nuclear clash with the United States—however wild her words—and understandably so.

We have the power not only to destroy completely her entire nuclear offensive forces but to devastate her society as well." Furthermore, should China be so "insane and suicidal" as to contemplate an attack upon the United States, there would be means available to her for which an ABM defense would be inadequate. There are many ways of overcoming such a defense. An ABM system would be ineffective against attack by means other than ICBMs—for example, low-flying aircraft, cruise missiles, missiles launched from offshore submarines, and missiles smuggled into ports from other locations and then detonated. In addition, there are a number of easy and inexpensive means by which an ICBM can penetrate an area defense such as the proposed system would provide for our cities. These penetration aids include fragmentation of the missile's booster rocket, chaff, decoys, electronic jamming, and radar blackout produced by the predetonation at high altitude of an incoming missile. All of these are relatively simple and at least some would be likely to be incorporated by an enemy whose initial ICBM deployment would be faced with an ABM. It would be naive to assume that a nation capable of the effort to produce an ICBM system would not add some such minor extra effort to its initial ICBM system if it is aware that it will be faced with an ABM system such as the proposed one.

The third stated objective was protection against ·the possibility of accidental attacks. An accidental attack is, by definition, an unintentional attack, and one might reasonably presume that a nation whose missile was accidentally fired would prefer to prevent its warhead from exploding upon an enemy target. A number of mechanical means are employed by the United States to reduce the likelihood of accidents, and it is reasonable to expect that safety measures are employed by other nations as well. Since the prevention of accidental attack is in the mutual interest of all nations involved, in exchange of the independent safety features employed by each nation should be possible, perhaps leading to a weapons-safety conference of the nuclear-weapon nations. An obvious additional desired feature would be to have provisions for the destruction or disarming of an accidentally fired missile by the nation to whom it belongs before such missile could reach its target. Senator Stuart Symington at the hearings before the disarmament subcommittee of the Senate Foreign Relations Committee suggested that we already can do this with our missiles. At the time of these hearings, both Secretary Laird and his deputy, David Packard, concurred in the view, but the Pentagon has since asked that their public testimony be changed to deny the possibility of disarming the missiles once fired. The difficulty with a destruct capability may be that one cannot prevent the nation under attack from triggering such a mechanism and so, for the purposes of having an assured deterrent, this destruct capability could present problems. Although I am generally not inclined to suggest purely technological solutions, it would seem that a tamper-proof destruct mechanism should be in the realm of technical feasibility. Along these lines, a suggestion to prevent unintentional or irrational firing of the Polaris submarine weapons could also safeguard against accidental firings as well. In 1964, a Permissive Action Link was suggested that would have provided a kind of electronic lock-up of the missiles, a lock-up that could be released only by radio signal from headquarters. This proposal was evidently dropped but might well be worth renewed consideration.

It is encouraging to note from the remarks in his announcement that the President is aware of some of the problems and dilemmas of the present arms balance. He noted that "there is no way that we can adequately defend our cities without a loss of life," stating in his announcement, "the heaviest defense system we consider, one designed to protect our major cities, still could not prevent a catastrophic level of United States fatalities from a deliberate all-out Soviet attack." At his press conference, he concluded that the only way we can save lives is to prevent war.

A significant point in the President's announcement was his continued emphasis on his desire to avoid programs that might be regarded as provocative to the Soviet Union. Under the present system of deterrence, this is a crucial point and one that we must not lose sight of. For most of the 1960's, we and the Soviet Union have maintained a strategic weapons relationship that can be characterized as one of stable deterrence. Under this relationship, both sides are assured that a nuclear attack by one side will be returned by a second-strike attack causing unacceptable damage to the initial attacker. This is so because both sides have sufficiently large and secure forces that even after being hit by a first-strike, significant residual retaliatory forces will remain. The recognition of this condition and the experience gained in living for several years under this condition have contributed to the stability of United States-Soviet Union military relations and to the relaxation of strategic tensions between the two superpowers. Anything that might threaten to alter this condition would be destablizing and a cause for increased tension. It is for this reason that provocative acts are to be avoided. This is as true for the Soviet Union as it is for the United States and should be as well-recognized by their leaders as it seems to be by ours. We would be doing ourselves as well as the Soviet Union a disservice to act on the supposition that they are being so foolhardy as to pursue a first-strike capability.

The proposed Safeguard system, whether regarded as provocative or not in its present form, leaves the door open to more provocative ABM steps on our part in the future. Unfortunately, the proposed "thin" ABM system with the annual review and evaluations suggested by the President can still be regarded as most likely a first step toward the construction of a thick system. What has happened in the past two months is that the Army was caught trying to take a giant step toward the thick system and has had to settle for presidential permission to take a small step instead.

In addition, there are other critical weapons decisions facing the President now. The most destabilizing strategic-weapons development in recent years has been the development of the Multiple Independently Targetable Re-entry Vehicle (MIRV), which will be ready for deployment within a few years. The deployment of MIRV in the absence of an extensive ABM on the other side would raise the specter of first-strike intentions. It is the ability to destroy with one of your missiles more than one of an opponent's missiles that puts a premium on striking first and hence is destabilizing. If the President sincerely wishes to avoid extreme provocation, he should make the decision now to refrain from testing, procurement, and deployment of MIRV. Continuing with MIRV cannot help but provoke the Soviet Union to expand both its offensive and defensive forces.

The President has put considerable emphasis in his announcement on prospective arms-limitation talks with the Soviet Union. If we are to move to an era of negotiation, as has been the President's pledge, it should be more fruitful if we do not use the tactics of confrontation as a bargaining ploy. If both sides are truly interested in halting the arms race, as seems to be the case, meaningful negotiations should proceed without introducing extraneous complicating factors, such as the Safeguard ABM Program. If we are to avoid proceeding beyond a point of no (or difficult) return, we must begin *now* to seek agreements. It is recognized that negotiations, of necessity, tend to be difficult and complex. However, once MIRV is fully developed and ready to deploy, the problems of controlling a strategic arms-limitation agreement become more severe. Therefore, it would be highly desirable to seek an *immediate* joint moratorium on the procurement and deployment of new strategic-weapons systems. This would include ABM, MIRV, and similar bomber systems. The moratorium should also include range testing of new missile systems, so as to stop MIRV before it is too late. Such a moratorium would afford the time and the atmosphere for achieving a more comprehensive agreement.

In the final analysis, the only permanent solution to the ABM and MIRV questions is a negotiated agreement limiting both defensive and offensive weapons systems. This must become the President's and the country's prime objective.

I would like now to discuss the areas of public concern and the ways in which ABM has become a public issue. The shifts of the Defense Department in their attempts to sell the nation on ABM has brought into serious question their credibility, which already had been brought into doubt as a result of the Vietnam war. The obvious reason for the Army's attempt to locate Sentinel sites near cities, when, under the concept of a thin area defense, the sites could have just as well been located several hundred miles from the cities, was that it would afford them an easier opportunity to proceed to a thick system, which appears to be their ultimate objective. The one-month period of review of the ABM question appears to have been used mainly as an attempt to cool public concern and outrage and to seek means by which a modified system could be made more palatable to the American public and Congress.

The shifting arguments and somewhat conflicting testimony of Secretaries Laird, Packard, and Rogers have done little to restore confidence in the administration's handling of this vital defense issue. The annual review of the ABM that the President proposes assures the proponents of an expanded ABM system ample opportunity to push their case on a regular and continuing basis. The history with regard to the ABM has shown that appropriate intelligence to support the Army position can be found or manufactured almost on demand. Thus, intelligence that the Soviet is continuing to increase their numbers of offensive weapons deployed will be the basis for demands to extend the number of ABMs protecting our land-based missiles, and any intelligence, regardless of how little substance, suggesting sophistication in the developing Chinese ICBMs will be used as strong arguments for expanding to a thick system around many of our cities. It is hard to imagine that the President would be able to withstand such future pressures since, in deciding to support an ABM system, he found it expedient to yield to military pressures even when there were strong Congressional and public forces operating in the opposite direction. It remains for the public to question and to apply pressure in order to contain Pentagon interests.

A second and perhaps most obvious reason for public interest is the huge amounts of money involved. At a time when our cities are deteriorating, people are going hungry, and our educational system is near collapse, tens of billions of dollars are spent on military systems without question of value or need. The threat to our country is not from foreign missiles but from a breakdown of our society from within. If there is to be a re-ordering of our national priorities, the public must take a hand. The ultimate aspect of public concern should be the arms race. The ABM issue may represent a final breakthrough in public awareness that the arms race must be a vital concern for everyone. It is hard to believe that we have lived with the threat of nuclear annihilation for more than 20 years and only now does the public seem to be aware and concerned about it. Previous issues of arms policy were never viewed in relation to the arms race but rather in terms of personal concerns with regard to fallout in the case of nuclear test-ban considerations and personal responses to the fallout-shelter program. For the first time, the arms race itself has become a matter of public concern and will have to remain so until it is ended or de-escalated.

I would like to conclude by discussing briefly the public role on these issues. If we consider the decision-making process in this country, we find that on defense issues the decision making takes place at a corporation level or above. Basically, a few large industrial concerns, the Pentagon, members of Congress, and the administration are involved and the public takes no or little part in such decisions. If there is a re-ordering of national priorities, the issues that would become important would include housing, welfare, education, and transportation. These are "people" issues and "people" would have to be involved in the de-cisions relating to them. However, unless we get this re-ordering of priorities, there will be little opportunity to address ourselves to these issues. It is, therefore, necessary that defense be made a "people" issue too. This suggests a positive action-oriented role for the public at large.

June 1969

FURTHER READING SUGGESTED BY THE AUTHOR:

ABM: Yes or No? by Donald Brennan, William O. Douglas, Leon Johnson, George S. McGovern, Jerome Wiesner, with an introduction by Hubert H. Humphrey (Santa Barbara, Calif.; Center for the Study of Democratic Institutions, 1969).

American Scientists and Nuclear Weapons Policy by Robert Gilpin (Princeton, N.J.: Princeton University Press, 1965).

Debate the Antiballistic Missile edited by Eugene Rabinowitch and Ruth Adams (Chicago: Bulletin of the Atomic Scientists, 1967).

NOTES ON CONTRIBUTORS

Jessie Bernard   "Comments on Report from Iron Mountain"

Professor of sociology, Pennsylvania State University.

Kenneth E. Boulding   "Comments on Report from Iron Mountain"

Professor of economics, Institute of Behavioral Science, University of Colorado. (For more detail, see the back cover.)

Leonard J. Duhl   "Comments on Report from Iron Mountain"

Special assistant to the Secretary, Department of Housing and Urban Development.

Irving Louis Horowitz   "Social Science Yogis and Military Commissars"

Professor of sociology and chairman of the department at Livingston College, Rutgers University. He is editor-in-chief of *Trans*-action and editor of *Studies in Comparative International Development.* Among his major books are *The Rise and Fall of Project Camelot, Professing Sociology, Three Worlds of Development* and most recently, *Masses in Latin America.*

Marvin Kalkstein   "ABM and the Arms Race"

Former chairman of the Federation of American Scientists and was chairman of that organization's committee on ABM. At the State University of New York at Stony Brook, he is associate professor of earth sciences; he also gives a course on arms control and disarmament issues in the department of political science.

Louis Kreisberg   "Non-Governmental Organizations"

Associate professor of sociology at Syracuse University and research associate at the Youth Development Center. His research has focused on poverty, fatherless families and public housing. He has edited *Social Processes in International Relations: A Reader.*

Raoul Naroll   "Does Military Deterrance Deter?"

Professor of anthropology, sociology and political science at Northwestern University. The study described in this article was part of Project Michaelson, a social science research project supported by the United States Navy as part of the Polaris submarine program.

Elwin H. Powell   "Paradoxes of the Warfare State"

Associate professor of sociology at the State University of New York at Buffalo. He is author of a forthcoming book, *The Design of Discord: Studies of Anomie.*

Marc Pilisuk   "Comments on Report from Iron Mountain"

Professor in residence, School of Social Welfare, University of California, Berkeley.

Anatol Rapoport   "Comments on Report from Iron Mountain"

Professor of mathematical biology, Mental Health Research Institute, University of Wisconsin.

John R. Raser   "The Failure of Fail-Safe"

Associate professor of international relations and government at the Claremont Graduate School and research associate and project director at the Western Behavioral Sciences Institute, La Jolla, California.

Milton Rosenberg   "New Ways to Reduce Distrust Between the United States and Russia"

Professor of psychology at the University of Chicago. A large part of his experimental work has focused on the process of attitude change.

Henry S. Rowen   "Comments on Report from Iron Mountain"

President, The RAND Corporation.

Bruce M. Russett   "Comments on Report from Iron Mountain"

Professor of political science, Yale University.

Murray Weidenbaum   "Comments on Report from Iron Mountain"

Assistant secretary for economic policy, United States Treasury Department.